The Archaeological Imagination

In memoriam

Ben Richard Sandford Cullen

1964–1995

As of the eighteenth century, he embodied
the archaeological imagination.

The Archaeological Imagination

Michael Shanks

Walnut Creek, California

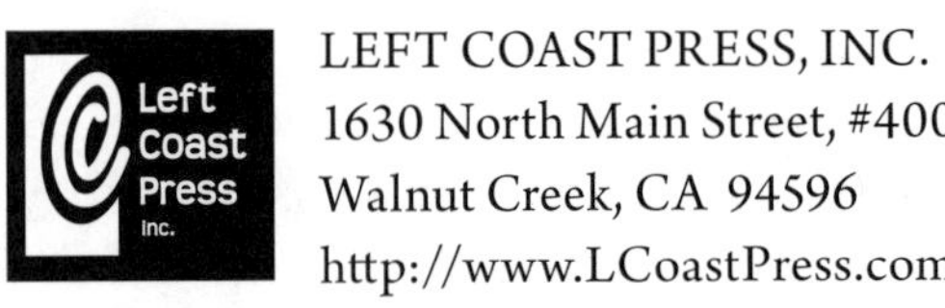

LEFT COAST PRESS, INC.
1630 North Main Street, #400
Walnut Creek, CA 94596
http://www.LCoastPress.com

ISBN 978-1-59874-361-6 hardcover
ISBN 978-1-59874-362-3 paperback
ISBN 978-1-61132-784-7 electronic

Library of Congress Cataloging-in-Publication Data:

Shanks, Michael.
The archaeological imagination / Michael Shanks.
p. cm.
Includes bibliographical references and index.
ISBN 978-1-59874-361-6 (hbk. : alk. paper)—ISBN 978-1-59874-362-3 (pbk. : alk. paper)—ISBN 978-1-61132-784-7 (ebook)
1. Archaeology–Philosophy. 2. Imagination. 3. Archaeology–Social aspects. 4. Archaeology–Methodology. 5. Archaeology–History. 6. Cultural property–Protection. 7. Antiquities–Collection and preservation. I. Title.
CC72.S49 2012
930.1–dc23

2011049564

Printed in the United States of America

⊗™ The paper used in this publication meets the minimum requirements of American National Standard for Information Sciences—Permanence of Paper for Printed Library Materials, ANSI/NISO Z39.48–1992.

Contents

Illustrations

Photographs and diagrams are by the author unless otherwise indicated.

Introduction

Archaeology fascinates us more than ever. The archaeologist is something of a romantic figure to be sure. Digging, discovering what was lost and forgotten, in the detective work of piecing together a picture or narrative of distant prehistoric pasts, of lost civilizations, through forensic traces of what happened, in a tangible connection between past and present, in an encounter with what is both familiar—lived lives and happenings that we can still understand, as well as with what is unfamiliar or exotic—events and ways of life changed even perhaps beyond comprehension. Archaeology encompasses passion for collection and fascination with senses of place rooted in the histories of people, and in evocation—past events associated with a particular site or building and still present in their traces. Then there is the sheer sense of mystery of ancient societies deep in an abyss of time and lit only dimly through their remains.

Archaeology has frequently accompanied high cultural conservatism. The connoisseur, for example, may celebrate ancient fine arts, the achievements of artisans patronized by the civilized wealthy and elite of the early imperial states, as great *human* achievements, quite separable from their social milieu. The conservationist may campaign

---

The Archaeological Imagination by Michael Shanks, 9–19.

to prevent the loss of cultural goods and the destruction of ancient sites in the face of a future-oriented contemporary will to economic growth and development. The nationalist may offer archaeological evidence for unbroken material continuity of heritage from the past in order to substantiate contemporary claims to territory and cultural identity. Here, though, there are equal opportunities for progressive political and cultural critique, for challenging orthodox or hegemonic historical narratives by grounding history in the remains of the past, the unedited evidence for past lives, rather than texts written by vested interests.

For the professional and academic archaeologist, the exigencies of legal compliance, teaching and grading student papers, managing and administering archaeological business, bidding for contract work, and hitting assessment targets for research publication may dampen all this intellectual and cultural ferment. Nonetheless, I know of no archaeologist who has come into the field to make a business fortune. Student surveys and evaluations over many years in the universities in which I have taught consistently confirm the force to motivate and inspire carried by such an archaeological agenda rooted in discovery, collection, senses of place and a contemporary romanticism.

And in what sense is the archaeologist a romantic figure? Surely the professional, in spite of popular media presentation, will not prefer melodrama over empirics, an investment in meticulous and painstaking systematized labor. But Romanticism, that European cultural movement of the eighteenth and nineteenth century, was an intimate component of those dynamic changes associated with enlightenment, reason and the experimental life, and challenges to religious teaching and the lineages of the absolutist state. Historians of archaeology have always located the beginnings of the modern discipline and profession in romantic nationalist movements of the first decades of modernity back in the nineteenth century and earlier, with new attitudes towards tradition, history and historical change, the nation states of Europe finding sources of identity and legitimation in an investigation of unwritten pasts, with those archaeological sources conspicuously displayed in the new museum institutions and their grand buildings in the capitals of the nineteenth century, and with those archaeological sites increasingly stewarded and visited in tourism and popular educational pursuits. In northern and western Europe, archaeology offered tangible traces of prehistoric antecedents to the world of Roman occupation: the ancient British, Celtic peoples, bronze age warrior societies, the megalithic monuments of early farming communities, back even to what is still sometimes seen as the origin of western art in the Palaeolithic cave paintings of southwestern France and northern Iberia. Little if any of this appeared in Greek and Roman historical accounts or in the biblical tradition of European Christianity, and the establishment of a long chronology for the earth and for humanity, way beyond the six thousand or so years that had elapsed since Creation, the chronology offered by orthodox biblical interpretation, opened up vast empty spaces of prehistoric time for which there were no historical accounts. The growing quantities of finds and sites that were of this great lacuna demanded attention, sorting and curation, and not least because these material remains, this archaeological heritage, was all that was left of the origins of the modern nation states of Europe.

This is all commonplace in accounts of the history of archaeology and will not be contentious, even to popular treatments in the mass media. What I suggest is less commonly discussed is the way ideologies such as romanticism and nationalism work through people's local and personal experiences, the character of the connections between popular romance and professional discipline, between the personal and subjective gratification offered by archaeology's experiences of the material past and its institutional, state sponsored locales. How do archaeological remains figure in debates about national and local identity? How does the romantic spectacle of ruin, increasingly popular from the eighteenth century, relate to careful scientific observation? How did personal memory, rooted in oral tradition, evolve with a critical apparatus of textual criticism and the investigation of material archaeological evidence? How does a visit to an archaeological site come to be connected with an experience of history?

This is the topic of this book: how archaeological themes are at the heart of our contemporary relationship with the past and its remains, how they resonate so well with broader cultural energies, and how to many this makes archaeology such an attractive field.

It was a fascination with Greco-Roman antiquity revealed through its ruins and remains that motivated my entry into academic archaeology; a commitment to new methods and theories of archaeological practice prompted me to shift attention to even more challenging uncertainty with research into early farming communities and their mortuary practices in northern Europe. In both I have felt keenly the obligation and responsibility borne by academics to reflect upon their practices and their connections with the communities that support their work (accepting that fortunate status of being able to pursue archaeological interests). Nearly forty years ago, in his much discussed article *Archaeology: the loss of innocence* in the journal *Antiquity* (1973), David Clarke argued that this obligation to critical self-consciousness followed from the development and maturity of the discipline; archaeologists were obliged to look to the history and theory of their practices in order to legitimate a claim to being worthy of academia. In our books in the 1980s (*ReConstructing Archaeology* and *Social Theory and Archaeology*) Chris Tilley and I went to great lengths to connect research into European prehistory with what can be called archaeology's *actuality,* its contemporary location today. So we connected museums, the media, academic archaeology, the heritage industry, social theory, and archaeological method with accounts of prehistoric monuments and pottery and even contemporary industrial design (beer cans) through a critique of archaeological practices in an overarching topic of archaeology's *cultural politics*.

In *Experiencing the Past* (1992) I widened my approach to this question of our motivation to pursue archaeological exploration and inquiry. What is archaeology? I took a pragmatic view and argued that archaeologists, like many others, simply work on what is left of the past. Proposition: to understand archaeology, consider the discipline's affinities. Looking out from the discipline, seeking connections in this genealogical investigation, involved unpacking common archaeological metaphors, such as digging deep for authenticity, and took me into discussion of how we document the past, visualization, forensics, the materiality of historical sources, rot and ruin, what happens to remains. I wasn't, at this stage, seeking the historical origins of such themes; instead I followed a kind of horizontal stratigraphy, an interpretive ethnography of archaeological practices and literatures, connecting the discipline and discourse of archaeology with personal experiences and memory practices, with the cultural dispositions of modernity. The topic then, and now in this book, is the origin of our modern and contemporary historical sensibilities or senses of history, senses of our place in history, the possibility of action that has historical effect. Strictly, because *origin* implies a singular source or invention, I should emphasize again that this is a *genealogical* quest for affinities and relationships.

The notion that this constituted an investigation of the archaeological imagination came soon after I joined the University of Wales Lampeter in 1992. The university was home to a new generation of human and cultural geographers, among them Chris Philo, Catherine Nash, Miles Ogborn, Tim Cresswell, Ulf Strohmayer (and more who had moved on or came later). The archaeologists, including Julian Thomas, Chris Tilley, David Austin, Martin Bell, Barry Burnham (and others, again who came later), were pursuing a program more interdisciplinary than was currently found in other UK universities. Lampeter's closely knit collegial environment fostered cross-disciplinary discussion. The archaeologists and geographers shared a common concern to bridge scientific and humanities approaches to the past and to space and landscape (recognizing old affinities between historical geography and archaeology), to reformulate our theories and methods such that they could encompass the human, experiential, subjective, *and* natural and objective aspects of human inhabitation, past and present. Some critics thought, erroneously, that this was about questioning the credentials of a scientific archaeology with an assertion of the creative and subjective. It was actually about probing the character of archaeological practices as science.

We were very conscious of the roots of our concern. While debates about theory and method were as old as sociology (and this book will take us back to the eighteenth century and earlier), we were working within a resurgence of debate that occurred with the growth of universities in Europe and the United States in the 1960s and after. C. Wright Mills published *The Sociological Imagination* in 1959, where he proposed a reconciliation of empiricism and theory, the individual and their social and cultural milieu, with sociology as a hybrid field, incorporating the biographical and historical as well as the social. I was especially interested in complementary efforts in European sociology to bring interpretive sensitivity to rigorous social science rooted in empirical substance: the critical theory of the post-war Frankfurt School was freshly available, and we were inspired by the likes of Theodor Adorno, Herbert Marcuse, Jürgen Habermas, as well as New-Left thinking in Britain, strongly rooted in the historiography of the likes of Eric Hobsbawm, Perry Anderson and E.P. Thompson. H.C. Prince, in an influential paper in the 1962 edition of the journal *Landscape,* had written of the essential aesthetic component of any appreciation of human habitat. The *geographical imagination,* as he saw it, was about *responses* to places and landscapes: their commingling of culture and nature prompts sympathetic insight and imaginative understanding. Prince emphasized the art of geographical *description,* throwing emphasis on the representation of land and habitat, on geo-*graphy,* the discursive or rhetorical features of the academic discipline. David Harvey had championed geography as spatial science in his *Explanation in Geography* of 1969 (in many ways a parallel to David Clarke's complex effort at an *Analytical Archaeology* in 1968), but made an about-face in 1973 with his *Social Justice and the City,* where he adopted a strident critique of positivist social science. Harvey's geographical imagination is a habit of mind that enables people to recognize the role of space and place in their own biographies, to creatively understand how spatial forms are fashioned and affect us. Then in 1994 Derek Gregory came out with his book *Geographical Imaginations.* Again the perspective was one that looked between and beyond academic disciplines, invoking issues that spiraled far beyond the discourse of the academy, bridging the personal, subjective, institutional and structural.

At the time, this effort to understand the history of human habitat and human being in a transdisciplinary milieu (and we did think that grandly!) involved both theoretical reflection and research case studies, mostly shared in academic seminars and papers. We began to talk about an archaeological imagination, along the lines of the sociological and geographical, as creative work on the remains of the past rooted in a faculty or sensibility dispersed through the cultural reception of the past. One line taken to expand debate, description and representation beyond academic language and writing, as implied by all the calls for *imagination,* was a phenomenological approach, emphasizing experience. I experimented in my book *Experiencing the Past* (1992) with narrative, imagery and models of how we connect with the past, including case studies of prehistoric monuments, Greek ceramic art, and medieval architecture. Tilley's 1994 *Phenomenology of Landscape,* on monumental responses to land in prehistory, was also precisely such an effort and has been very influential, though the degree to which he managed to escape academic discourse and discussion was limited (consider also a later effort with Sue Hamilton, Barbara Bender and Ed Anderson—*Stone Worlds,* 2007).

For me, a new line of exploration of the archaeological imagination came again in Lampeter with a relationship struck up with the arts and performance company *Brith Gof.* Conscious of Lampeter's embrace of themes that reached beyond the academy, especially concerning the reception of the past and as explored in my book *Experiencing the Past,* Mike Pearson and Cliff McLucas, artistic directors of this theater company, approached our department looking for collaboration. They specialized in multimedia site specific works that dealt with memory, place and belonging. In a series of joint works we combined academic research and archival sources with scenography, dramaturgy and performance at larger and smaller scales in specific places that were culturally and historically charged. *Tri Bywyd* (*Three Lives*) (1995), for example, was set in a ruined farmstead buried deep in a state-run forest plantation created by the compulsory purchase and forced eviction of local families. The performance over three nights and subsequent documentation (in Nick Kaye's book *Site-Specific Art* Of 2000) combined three deeply researched dossiers of local Welsh lives and deaths. Prominent was the theme of how the same evidence, record and archive can prompt quite different interpretation and account—how social location and what may be called forensic politics influence representation. Other projects used artworks as a kind of ethnographic or cultural probe, in McLuhan's sense: presenting work that would precipitate reaction and reflection upon our topic of the place of the past in the present. The collaboration culminated in a book *Theatre/Archaeology* (with Mike Pearson, 2001) and a research project, *Three Landscapes,* hosted by the Stanford Humanities Center in 2000. These and other similar projects in the archaeological imagination are quite well covered online and are easily found through any Web search engine.

Alain Schnapp's researches into the history of archaeology, notably and beautifully presented in *The Discovery of the Past* (English translation 1996), have provided new ground for exploring the roots of the archaeological imagination. The intellectual world of the antiquarian, before the consolidation of academic disciplines in the nineteenth century, was one that allowed traverse across many disparate fields of research, learning and practice. Antiquarian interests in collecting antiquities and documenting landscape and community could combine artifact study with human geography, toponymy, genealogy, natural history, and whatever else that seemed appropriate to an antiquarian to include. Antiquarians—practicing clerics, lawyers, diplomats, or just plainly of independent means—were central to the development of experimental science as well as art history. These pre-disciplinary connections are provocative case studies that allow us to control for the later crystallization of disciplinary institutions: they are kind of counterfactuals, posing questions such as—What if we didn't have disciplines? What then would the study of material remains look like? How can science and art be combined in rigorous study and reconstruction (of the past)?

In the ways just described, the archaeological imagination is a bridging field, connecting different ways of working on remains of the past. Considering the roots of the archaeological imagination in antiquarianism, as I do in this book, also points to the convergence of prediscisciplinary and postdisciplinary practice, common ground shared between seventeenth and eighteenth century intellectuals, unencumbered by modern academic disciplines, and the twenty-first century field of research and design. Many universities the world over are promoting interdisciplinary initiatives, because the most interesting questions and tough real-world problems are messy and don't fit neatly into academic disciplines. Major investment in bio-technology, sustainable economic policy, international relations, cultural development, and healthcare research necessitates post-disciplinary thinking and project management. All these fields include pure and applied science, technology, and a fundamental human component, cultural as well as behavioral. The demand to be open and interdisciplinary was anticipated by antiquarians and others in the modern Enlightenment and earlier days of the development of experimental science. I have been much influenced by the research of historians of science, such as Steven Shapin and Simon Schaffer in their book *Leviathan and the Air Pump* (1986), that shows the fundamental intellectual and cultural connections across fields now widely separated, as in their examples of the political philosophy of Thomas Hobbes and the chemistry of Robert Boyle.

Notions of the archaeological, sociological, and geographical imagination all imply *creative* understanding of life today, of possibilities of change, innovation, of the roles of individual perception, practice and agency. Widely separated fields of life and experience need connecting. At Stanford we include these aspirations in the mission and programs of our *d.school* (the Hasso Plattner Institute of Design). The connection between an archaeological imagination and the field of human-centered design will be clearer if I introduce again my simple definition of archaeology that does not assume the discipline—archaeologists *work* with the remains of the past, acting on and through artifacts, making interventions in the land through fieldwork and excavation, producing collections, authoring accounts and narratives, producing books and papers, performing talks and lectures, building museums and institutions. The archaeological imagination is creative and constitutive. Design thinking, as we call it in the d.school, is focused on the practices of making, authoring, and creating, and includes the application of imagination to intervene in the structures of everyday and individual realities, to connect perceptions and the cultural imaginary, in making artifacts and experiences that will enhance human life. The craft of archaeology, working on the reception of the past through remains of all kinds, is included, by definition, *a priori*.

I owe a tremendous debt to friends and colleagues who have also reflected upon archaeological motivations and connections. The literary and cultural ground of the archaeological imagination has been best explored. David Lowenthal's *The Past is a Foreign Country* (1985) is a magisterial miscellany of examples. Jennifer Wallace has written a personal and insightful study of literary treatments of archaeological metaphors in *Digging the Dirt* (2004). Christine Finn's *Past Poetic: Archaeology and the Poetry of W.B. Yeats and Seamus Heaney* (2004) is complemented by her fascinating application of the archaeological imagination to contemporary hi-tech industries in *Artifacts: An Archaeologist's Year in Silicon Valley* (2002). Other studies include Kitty Hauser's *Shadow Sites: Photography, Archaeology, and the British Landscape* 1927–1955 (2007); Eric Downing's *After Images: Photography, Archaeology, and Psychoanalysis and the Tradition of Bildung* (2006); and a very useful collection edited by Brian Neville and Johanne Villeneuve, *Waste-Site Stories: The Recycling of Memory* (2002). The journal *Modernism/Modernity* ran a special issue in 2004 on *Archaeologies of the Modern* (edited by Jeffrey Schnapp, Matthew Tiews and myself): included were a wide range of case studies of modernity seen through an archaeological lens. A related book is Julian Thomas's *Archaeology and Modernity* (2004).

I have already mentioned the work of Alain Schnapp on the history of archaeology; keep a lookout for his forthcoming study of ruins in the archaeological imagination, and the publication of his project that coordinates a cross-cultural and comparative history of antiquarian thought. A superb account of the world of one antiquarian is Peter Miller's *Peiresc's Europe: Learning and Virtue in the Seventeenth Century* (2000). Sam Smiles's *The Image of Antiquity: Ancient Britain and the Romantic Imagination* (1994) is also very thoughtful and thought provoking. In contrast to this kind of scholarship, Ronald Jessup produced a quirky collection of quotes and incidents from the history of archaeology in *Curiosities of British Archaeology* (1961).

On archaeology and the media and popular receptions of the archaeological past, Cornelius Holtorf has written two studies, *Stonehenge to Las Vegas: Archaeology as Popular Culture* (2005), and *Archaeology Is a Brand!: The Meaning of Archaeology in Contemporary Popular Culture* (2007). There is also a recent collection, *Archaeology and the Media,* edited by Timothy Clack and Marcus Brittain (2007). In contrast to these archaeology-centered approaches is Siegfried Zielinski's *Deep Time of the Media: Toward an Archaeology of Hearing and Seeing by Technical Means* (2006)—offering up the field of *media archaeology,* extending archaeology as a concept to media devices and experiences. Bill Rathje also extended archaeological thinking to contemporary society in his pioneering foundation of *garbology,* the anthropology of garbage: a great summary is his book with Cullen Murphy, *Rubbish!: The Archaeology of Garbage* (1992).

A most subtle and powerful work that takes us into the kind of archaeological imagination represented by the great Marxian critic Walter Benjamin is Laurent Olivier's wonderful *Le Sombre Abîme du Temps: Memoire et Archéologie* (2008, English translation 2012), where he associates archaeology with Bergson's temporality of duration—what I take up in this book as *actuality.* This kind of treatment also offers a segue into another application of the term archaeology to historiography, as, notoriously of course, in the work of Michel Foucault (*The Order of Things* and *The Archaeology of Knowledge,* English translations 1969 and 1972).

Thanks are due to all those who have responded to my talks and classes and to the rambling ruminations offered in my Website and

Weblog, *mshanks.com* and *michaelshanks.org*. The collective photography site *archaeography.com* is a very stimulating environment at the limits of the archaeological imagination. These sites are springboards for exploring the extraordinary fertility of the archaeological imagination in contemporary art, as well as photography.

1. We Are All Archaeologists Now

1.1 *Sensibility and Imagination*

This is a book about the fascination of archaeology, about archaeological ways of looking and thinking about things.

I take a broad view of archaeology, and include not only the academic discipline, a field of university and museum-based research and teaching centered upon material remains, but also cultural resource management, the management of sites and artifacts according to what is now a global system of legal instruments and agreements designed to protect the past, and the heritage industry of museums and protected sites that figure, for example, so prominently in tourism. Then there are the intangible aspects of archaeology: the evocation of ruin, authenticity achieved through digging deep.

The topic, as I aim to show, is the reception of the past in all its manifestations, though archaeology is not inappropriately taken as dealing with material remains. Archaeology, as an academic discipline,

The Archaeological Imagination by Michael Shanks, 21–42.

involves issues of scholarship and rigor in managing *the archaeological process,* which I summarize simply as working on what is left of the past. Archaeology, as well as a way of thinking about the past (in the present), is work that requires resources, and this implies what might be called a political economy, ways of organizing and managing the means of pursuing archaeological interests—institutions such as universities and museums, systems of authority, command and control, funding mechanisms that put people and their tools and instruments in the field to dig, survey, record, remove.

Mention of political economy, institutions, authority and control may seem to signal a dry approach to the topic of the fascination of archaeology. It is, and I will not be tackling these matters directly, but they really are vital and engaging. Gaining access to the past, finding the means to tell one's own story of origin and belonging can be a contentious matter in what Robert Hewison, back in 1987, termed the *heritage industry.* This is part, in turn, of that phenomenon that saw considerable growth through the twentieth century, *the culture industry,* offering goods and experiences for entertainment, edification, and profit. Archaeology as a discipline emerged as part of old European and indeed Asian traditions of antiquarian interests and pursuits: collecting old and valued artifacts, and producing regional accounts of a community's character and history through its monuments, landscapes, family genealogies, geography. Collection, documentation, and identity remain key components of an archaeological aspect of the heritage industry. A visited site may be said to offer direct access to a particular archaeological history of a people or community: *their own* heritage. The archaeological process in a general sense, focused on material traces, has long proved evocative, lending itself to many fertile associations and metaphors: the archaeologist as detective, fieldwork and discovery, digging deep to find what may provide a key to contemporary concerns.

A focus on archaeological process is not meant to detract from *the object of archaeology*: to gain knowledge through ruins and remains of societies and cultures similar and different to our own; to build models and narratives of how they lived; to investigate the great changes in human history—community, civilization, empire; to determine the shape of human evolution, assessing the forces that drive history and structure our lives, delving into the very character of human being.

Means and methods of accessing people's pasts, understanding where we have come from and how. This is quite an intoxicating prospect!

Rather than continue with this conventional introduction of archaeological process and object, let me begin again in what may appear to be a more oblique way, as a means of introducing the notion of the archaeological *imagination*.

Anselm Kiefer is a contemporary artist. His work is, I suggest, a profound application of an archaeological sensibility. *Die Ordnung der Engel* (The Hierarchy of Angels) (1985 to 1987) is a massive wall-sized canvas of thick layers of paint, shellac, chalk, and cardboard. A large airplane propeller, worn, broken, made from sheets of lead, sits on a dark, blasted, eroded, and barren landscape, from which hang nine rocks. In a text of the fifth century entitled *The Celestial Hierarchy,* attributed to Dionysius the Areopagite, angels were divided into nine categories or choirs, grouped into three hierarchies, navigating the twisting space between heaven and earth. The propeller, spiraling through the air, the airpower of Germany's Third Reich, or any twentieth-century military might, now brought down to burned earth, references Dionysius's vision of heaven as a vast spiral, a topological folding in which time and space move in all directions. The rocks, as meteorites, as angels, bring heaven to earth, to a wasted utopia in this representation of a different kind of celestial hierarchy.

Since the 1970s Kiefer has dealt in the cultural landscapes of postwar Germany, with mixed media works manifesting the transmutation of materials, through references to burning and devastation, death and decay, erosion and ruin, the metamorphosis of substance, lead into gold, in the celestial models of alchemy. In some of Kiefer's work grand architectural and public monuments—ancient, Egyptian, classical, industrial—signal imperial ambition, the nation state; other locales remind us of the architectures of the Holocaust. Several series of books, with pages of text often eroded and undecipherable, of faded anonymous photographs, of empty pages, burned books, seem to be a melancholic kind of literary antiquarianism. All his work embodies complex allegories that draw on Jewish mysticism, Christian symbolism, folk legend, and, as in *Die Ordnung der Engel,* Kiefer displays his fascination with alchemical systems of thought that obsessed so many great minds before the triumph of an enlightenment will to knowledge—worlds of faith, superstition, ritual and hope. In Barjac, France, Kiefer converted an abandoned silk factory and surroundings into a 35 hectare environment, a total art work (*Gesamtkunstwerk*) of glass buildings, archives, installations, storerooms for materials and paintings, subterranean chambers and corridors.

Kiefer has persistently worked on the legacy, in Germany particularly, of the Second World War, addressing the famous question posed by Theodor Adorno of how can there be poetry after Auschwitz, exploring in his own dark art that interpenetration of reason, hope and horror that was the subject of Adorno and Horkheimer's *Dialectic of Enlightenment,* published at the beginning of the Second World War, outlining the failure of reason since antiquity, the consequences of reason, the deep genealogy of modernity's totalitarian nightmare.

Questions of tradition and legacy, of heritage, of roots, memories and remains, of entropy and loss, the material transformation of decay and ruin, connections between the past, its contemporary reception, and future prospect, the place of the past in a modern society, ethical and indeed political issues regarding respect for the past and the conservation of its remains, agency and the shape of history, but also judgment of responsibility in assessing what to do with what is left of the past: these are all components of an archaeological sensibility at the heart of Kiefer's art. I hope it is clear that they also have wide valency.

By sensibility I mean ways of perceiving, awareness, cultural and cognitive, across all the senses; an emotional consciousness and recognition of a fact or a condition of things. I have used Kiefer as an example of an archaeological sensibility, because I think some of the richest explorations of the archaeological imagination are to be found in contemporary art, as a kind of barometer of contemporary cultural dispositions. So, in the dark light of Kiefer's art, and with reference to my opening topics of archaeological process and archaeological object, let me offer a definition of the archaeological imagination:

> To recreate the world behind the ruin in the land, to reanimate the people behind the sherd of antique pottery, a fragment of the past: this is the work of the archaeological imagination, a creative impulse and faculty at the heart of archaeology, but also embedded in many cultural dispositions, discourses and institutions commonly associated with modernity. The archaeological imagination is rooted in a sensibility, a pervasive set of attitudes towards traces and remains, towards memory, time and temporality, the fabric of history.

Where do we typically see this work of the archaeological imagination? In museums; in collections and archives of all kinds; in the application by government and non-government agencies of legislation to protect the archaeological past; in the ways that memory reaches back to connect traces of the past with something in the present that has sparked the effort of re-collection; in efforts to preserve and conserve the past, whether this be a site or an artifact; in reconstructions and reenactments of the past, whether this be in photorealistic virtual reality or in the performances of enthusiasts in medieval costume and character at a Renaissance Fair. A mobile team of metaphors offers articulatory force: digging deep through layers to find an answer, the human mind being organized, according to Freud, a passionate collector of antiquities, in stratified layers, just like an archaeological site; fieldwork as forensic detection; ruin and decay as cultural decline and loss; the remains of the past as a core to one's identity, personal and cultural.

There is a paradox or tension at the heart of an archaeological sensibility: a fascination with things, with material goods, with collection, accompanies a kind of contempt for their base materiality (see Olsen, Shanks, Webmoor, Witmore 2012). Our modern world abounds in *material things*, and yet the academic Humanities and

Arts, and high culture more generally, consistently privilege *immaterial cultural values*. In this paradigmatic split, artistic genius, for example, may be seen as manipulating a medium into an artwork that *expresses* human values, sentiment, experience. Science, math and physics, engineering and materials science seem opposed, with their focus on the natural world, to what is usually held to be the heart of the human condition—such immaterial sentiment. I will be exploring this familiar dualism particularly as it connects with the mortality of human corporeality, with human experiences of time. For while dates of events are clearly important to archaeological and historical accounts, the time of archaeology is distinctively concerned more with what remains, with *what becomes of what was*, with the way the past hangs on, lingers, is lost, or may be collected and cared for, left as legacy. Such engagements with duration are the kind of relationship between past and present at the heart of heritage.

1.2 *The Genealogy of a Sensibility*

What has engendered this archaeological sensibility? What supports the work of the archaeological imagination? What are their origins?

One somewhat tautological or circular answer is that the archaeological imagination accompanies those institutions and structures that I listed at the end of the introduction as part of contemporary memory practices: museums and archives, collections, archaeological research, the work of government planning departments and ministries of culture in their work of heritage management. In this answer the archaeological imagination is an emergent feature of a particular *ecology of practices*. I borrow this term from Isabelle Stengers (2005 and 2010); it refers to a particular community and its unique *habitat*. It complements the Foucauldian notion of structures of discourse that enable the production of archaeological knowledge (as discussed in Shanks 1992 and 1996). Here I use the term to encompass infrastructures (museum collections, map rooms, spaces of interaction for antiquarians and archaeologists, libraries, laboratories), instruments, vocabulary, media, and other diverse interlocutors, which are gathered around a particular matter of concern, in this case the (material) presence of the past. An ecology of practices is more than descriptive. It intervenes. It aims, as Stengers puts it, "at the construction of new 'practical identities' for practices, that is, new possibilities for them to be present, in other words to connect" (2005, 186). The archaeological imagination, it can be argued, is an emergent property of this project, initiated in the seventeenth and eighteenth centuries, to forge new engagements between the past and the present.

I am certainly going to argue that the archaeological imagination is part of our modernity, but I don't want to treat it as an aspect of something like a contemporary *zeitgeist*, or spirit of our modern times. Lowenthal (1985), Wallace (2004) and Holtorf (2005, 2007) have written compilations along these lines, more descriptive than analytical, where they give many examples of the reception of the material past and the work of archaeology in popular and high culture. Instead of such static pictures, I want to offer a more dynamic *genealogy*, tracking connections back to the beginnings of modernity in the seventeenth century and earlier, offering a treatment of the archaeological imagination that *explains* as well as outlines its origin and the forms it takes (and hence my reference to that notion of an ecology of practices offered by Stengers). Kiefer presents reflections upon the fabric of history, experiences, responsibilities and culpabilities under a longer term view that reaches back to systems of arcane knowledge and cosmogonies, to folk traditions that predate the consolidation of our modern academic disciplines and systems of knowledge. This reaching back and tracking of lines of descent from earlier to later systems of thought and practice counterposes alternatives to the scientific application of reason, so familiar in systems of knowledge since the eighteenth century. I will identify a particular fulcrum of creativity and the imagination—matters of the creation of history, our own history, histories imposed upon us, in the context of loss and ruin, as well as cosmologies and systems of order; the genealogy of the archaeological imagination is about ways that Science and matters usually reserved for the Humanities can be profoundly complementary.

In respect of such deep anxieties as displayed in the work of Kiefer's archaeological imagination, I want to begin with a particular aspect of this question of the origin of an archaeological sensibility and ask—what has happened to tradition?

I live in Silicon Valley where information and communications technology companies, with their aggressively entrepreneurial start-up culture, could hardly be more future-oriented. Venture capital funding hinges on calculating risk and future return. Development and growth are premised upon innovation, shedding the constraints of conventional ways of doing things. Patent also is a distinctively Californian, countercultural, and indeed utopian desire to create a new and better world. The Valley itself has changed enormously in the last forty years, most of the groves of fruit trees gone in urban development that stretches fifty miles and more beyond San Francisco and San José. There is an intense concern with what this means for local community identity. Palo Alto, in the heart of Silicon Valley, once a part of small-town America, is now a model of a new kind of industrial urbanism at the heart of the new technology and knowledge industries (see Peter Hall's great account in his *Cities in Civilization*, 2001). The community embodies these tensions. IT affluence regularly results in older buildings being targeted for teardown; the city is a desirable zip code, but its smaller older houses and properties don't always appeal to new interests and developer profit-seeking. Nevertheless, stringent building codes prohibit any major and even many minor alterations of properties older than fifty years. Newly-old downtown commercial buildings are protected, even though they are hardly notable as examples of modern or vernacular architecture; eyesores are a key to physiognomic character. IDEO, a large design consultancy, has its Palo Alto studios in several converted light industrial units, including what was Earl Ellison's *Repair and Radiator Company*, established in 1929. The building now sports a fine yellow "Ellison's" sign specially made to replace the one lost when the building was refurbished in 2000, and IDEO had to comply with the tight regulations that aim to conserve the traces of the local past. Across the road is a mundane concrete base of a column that had lain in the undergrowth by the sidewalk until it was "restored" and given pride of place at the entrance to an underpass to the new medical center.

I suggest this articulation of radical development and change with an attention to local history is commonplace. What brings together this cultural neurosis over the loss and preservation of the past with an orientation to the future and a faith in technology and reason? Let me now take up a broad brush and sketch some features of the reconfiguration of historical roots since the seventeenth and eighteenth centuries, the decline and restitution of traditions, combined with radical focus on calculating futures.

Most academic disciplines are deeply divided fields of argument and uncertainty; this can make them quite stimulating—the big interesting questions seem to remain forever unanswered, and very much so in the Humanities and Social Sciences. Archaeologists vigorously debate theory and method, as well as accounts offered of the likes of the origins of agriculture, the origins of civilization and complex society, the role of traded goods in ancient empires, the reasons for collective burial in prehistoric monuments. These arguments are like storms in a teacup compared with a broader sense of crisis facing the archaeological past in the present. There are today unprecedented threats to the material past, enormous challenges of managing the loss, of mitigating the impacts on archaeological sites coming from urban and rural development. Looting and the illicit trade in antiquities destroy whole sites and ancient landscapes. Legal apparatuses are needed to regulate competing claims on historical roots, on past legacies, when history may become conflated with heritage, and even the recent past can take on considerable cultural value, as in my example from Palo Alto. We now have a whole new field focused on the ethics and politics of property-seen-as-heritage, covering matters of rights and responsibilities to the past, the reconciliation of opportunity, threat and stakeholder interests.

This discourse of threat and loss goes back to the nineteenth and eighteenth centuries. Industrialization and urbanization have brought colossal cultural displacement, creating whole new classes and communities that do not inherit a long-standing or traditional relationship with the past. The modern disciplines of history, archaeology and anthropology have offered means of holding on to what was changing, means of curating the past and connecting with the future, through visions and narratives of progress, of improvement, or of simply understanding where we have come from. In place of traditional accounts, archaeology and historiography provide orientation substantiated by research. This academic and intellectual field is part of a broader modernist sensibility that deals in the decline of tradition, the rise of historical sensibilities attuned to social and cultural change as well as tradition, that appreciate the remains of the past and of other cultures, housed in the new architectures of the museum and increasingly protected by institutions of the nation state. This modernist historicity, or sense of the historical past, includes attention to the flow of events and personalities, social change, and individual agency, or indeed human mortality in the face of the tide of history.

Though there are these deeper roots, two centuries old, as I will later illustrate, what is typically called *Cultural Resource Management* has seen exponential growth since the 1970s. At first in the 1960s growing perception of threats to the remains of the past prompted programs of "rescue" and "salvage" archaeology, mostly in the United States and the UK, with visions of the remains of the past rescued from beneath the developers' bulldozers. Since then, and aided by various legal and legislative instruments, there has been a shift of emphasis to the management or stewardship of valued sites and artifacts under a sense of ethical responsibility to future generations. This is now a global phenomenon, with prominent recognition coming from the likes of UNESCO, and indeed the World Bank, in its acknowledgement of the crucial role of culture in economic development. Of note also is the convergence of concern about cultural as well as natural resources, indeed a convergence that pertinently questions the very distinction.

Clearly, the quickening pace of urban and industrial development over the last fifty years has had a tremendous impact on archaeological remains, prompting the legislative and state interventions. The past itself seems under threat; at the minimum it needs protection. Archaeology, as a mode of appropriation and engagement with the past, is a component of a now global and hegemonic academic culture industry, with comparable curricula and discourse found in every university the world over. The archaeological past of sites, monuments and works housed in museums is at the heart of the tourist industry and features prominently in popular mass media. Archaeology and archaeological awareness is more than ever obviously wrapped up in contemporary (post)modernity.

In his lifelong project of writing a history of archaeology, culminating in the book *A History of Archaeological Thought* (1989 and later editions), Bruce Trigger successfully connected the discipline with broad modernist trends in nationalism, imperialism and colonialism. Archaeology has indeed grown as part of ways that modern industrial states develop senses of national identity, especially in relation to other cultures, encountered in the growing global market as well as in imperial expansion and colonization. Julian Thomas has connected archaeological thinking more broadly with modern ideologies (in *Archaeology and Modernity*, 2004). Both Trigger and Thomas have focused on archaeology as an academic discipline and profession, and both consider archaeology as a coherent disciplinary field, as do all histories of archaeology. Here I wish to turn things round somewhat and, instead of starting with archaeology the discipline, look at how broad changes over the last couple of hundred years have involved an archaeological sensibility that has prompted and enabled the success of disciplines like archaeology, history, and indeed anthropology.

To this end, I suggest that it is useful to treat this sense of crisis concerning the past as an archaeological manifestation of what is being called "risk society" (Shanks and Witmore 2009). The term was first developed by Ulrich Beck (*Risk Society: Towards a New Modernity*, 1992) and Anthony Giddens (*Modernity and Self-Identity : Self and Society in the Late Modern Age*, 1991) and describes escalating shifts in modernity centered upon concern with manufactured risks and threats. Giddens emphasizes changes that involve an end of tradition, in the sense of the past no longer being guarantor of contemporary security, in the sense that individuals are increasingly held responsible for their own security in a world experienced as more and more subject to risks to self, family and community.

Peter Sloterdijk (in *Sphären III –Schäume, Plurale Sphärologie,* 2004) and Michel Serres (in *The Natural Contract,* 1995) flag up growing senses of threat to global humanity's very habitat and survival—atmosphere, food and sustenance, water and housing. We are no longer simply subject to fate and nature: the cumulative effect of certain behaviors, policies and values is having deleterious effect on the stability of our human cultural ecology. Considerable attention is given to the implication of individuals, institutions and corporations in changes that seem to threaten the very core of human being: the engineering of genetic change, environmental change, the instabilities of a global monetary economy, international (in)security in the face of terrorism and nuclear proliferation. And the loss of the past, associated with changes in the way history itself is conceived and experienced.

Connecting archaeology with such an analysis of risk society locates an archaeological sensibility primarily outside the academy. Changes in archaeological thought, I am arguing, are a fundamental component of contemporary memory practices that have a *particular* manifestation in the academy and its discourses. Memory practices are a primary feature of the archaeological imagination. Archives and collections are an obvious manifestation—ways of organizing and physically accessing the past, without any necessary reference to a narrative or linear timeline, it should be noted. Archives are relational and multidimensional collocations, offering the *possibility* of access, if so desired, but by no means requiring anything more than the labor of maintaining the links and physically conserving the archival content. Such memory practices are modes of articulating past and present, with concomitant ethical issues of responsibilities, or not, to the preservation or conservation of cultural heritage.

Consider also the growth of garbology (the social-scientific study of garbage, after Bill Rathje) and the archaeology of the *contemporary* past, stretching archaeological interests in directions inconceivable, or at best marginal, a few decades ago. Consider how there is a new shape to the scope of archaeological inquiry, with acceptance of the crucial relevance of long term archaeological process to the understanding of climate change, to human interventions in the environment, to the development of state and empire, to communication, travel and mobility (what Giddens subsumes under his term *time-space distanciation*). Thirty years ago, when I was starting out in an archaeological career in the academy, there simply was no scope or agenda for questioning the value-freedom of (social) science, for debating the politics of the archaeological past, for treating pasts forged in the present in association with cultural struggles for genuine local identity in an increasingly globalist and neoliberal world, for locating archaeology in these contemporary forces (cf. Shanks and Tilley 1987a and 1987b). Quite appropriately, archaeology and Cultural Resource Management were embedded in long-standing agendas to establish a coherent time-space systematics for both the management of endangered sites and finds as well as for academic research, and to harness the power of quantitative social science for modeling social change. They were, and still largely are, part of that broad modernist program instituted particularly from the early nineteenth century and typically involving abstract expert systems that permit disembedded comparison and calculation across indefinite time and space.

The development of such large scale abstract systems of knowledge acquisition and management related to the monitoring and direction of everyday life has been amply explored after the likes of Foucault and his commentators. I find particularly interesting Mary Poovey's book titled *A History of the Modern Fact* (1998), which tracks changes in how knowledge was produced and substantiated from sixteenth century double-entry bookkeeping to nineteenth century statistics, covering, along the way, the relationship between observation and theory, particular facts and explanatory systems. Focused on everything from medicine to criminology, economy and environment, state directed and coordinated through bureaucracies, markets and all kinds of research agencies, including the academy, colossal resources have been given over to surveillance, measurement and analysis, with the aim of regulation and control. The building of these knowledge-based systems has involved the development of instruments and techniques of observation and measurement such as cartography and photography, standards and infrastructures that facilitate comparison and analysis, statistics operating upon databases, as well as institutions and management structures that allow the translation of observation into data into information into policy into execution. The result is society focused on control.

If all of human life and experience is in principle calculable and subject to knowledge, that we might understand better the likely outcomes of particular actions, attention is thrown onto the future because some sort of assessment of likely risks can be made for virtually all habits and activities; this is the core now of healthcare industries, financial services, insurance, all the way to government policies. These abstract and comparative knowledge systems throw suspicion on traditional answers and precepts in favor of research and analysis oriented toward the future and implying assessment of threats and opportunities. Hence the notion of risk is central in a society which is taking leave of the past, of traditional ways of doing things, and which is opening itself up to a problematic future.

This is part of the wholesale reorientation of temporality so central to modernity and which, of course, encompasses the likes of cultural resource management and archaeology. Challenges to senses of history based upon religious teaching, biblical chronologies and Graeco-Roman historiography, and, by the end of the eighteenth century, the establishment in geology of the deep antiquity of the earth, meant that most of human history appeared newly empty and only accessible through the archaeological remains of pre-history, or through analogy with contemporary simpler and traditional societies. Archaeology has worked successfully over two centuries to populate these great voids in human history. Excavation, survey, fieldwork and collection have thrown up and brought to attention ever growing quantities of data from the past that cannot be assimilated by the old traditional accounts of human history. The challenge has been how to handle this historical debris: a question of responsibility to order and comprehend. Museologists, from Thomsen and Worsaae in the 1840s onwards, have adopted a solution that connects well established but hitherto conjectural histories of humankind (evolutionary sequences from primitive stone age through bronze and iron using complex societies) with administrative technologies. Databases and inventory systems mobilize these schemes of historical development and change, and are organized, literally, through bureaucracy: the drawers, cupboards, cases and tables of museum galleries and storerooms offer ordered containers for the remains of the past.

So archaeological sites and artifacts have come to be organized in a global time-space systematics of timelines and distribution maps rooted in universally applicable systems of classification and categorization and embodied in the fittings and architecture of museums. This inventory of archaeological remains has become the foundation and instrument of the management of the past in ministries of culture and planning departments the world over. This system of order has nevertheless, indeed necessarily, come with a growing awareness of threats both to the remains of the past and to the possibility of creating any kind of meaningful knowledge of what happened in history. This is because these systems make very clear the implications for knowledge of lack of historical sources, of restricted access to data, gaps in the record, of inadequate care for what has been collected, of the loss of contextual information.

Here we experience a new kind of threat or risk to the past itself, as well as to the possibility of creating rich histories in the future. These administrative systems introduce a new dynamic between presence and absence, between the presence of the remains of the past gathered in museums, and the absence of past lives themselves, between archaeological finds and vast aeons of human history begging to be filled with what has been lost or is forever gone. In contrast to societies that experience the security of tradition, a past that serves as a reference for the present, the past in a "risk society" is conspicuously not a secure given at all. It is subject to contemporary interests and concerns, infused with the interests of knowledge, a will to knowledge, and also with erosive threatening interests. We have become aware that we need to work on the past simply to have it with us; if nothing is done, it may well disappear, especially when some want to break it up and sell it off to collectors or to build a new shopping mall. Just as the natural environment is not now seen as a given, but as a thoroughly socialized and institutionalized habitat, a hybrid that includes threats, culpability, and responsibility on the part of humanity to care and curate, so, too, the past is a matter of concern, a matter demanding foresight, another risk environment affecting whole populations' needs and desires for history, heritage, memory that offer orientation as much to the future as to the past.

Here we see how archaeology is quite different from historiography, in relation to the character of the sources upon which they work, their ontology. Archaeology, in working on material remains of the past in the present, is focused first upon duration and persistence, the entropic processes according to which the past is lost, and other processes that arrest decay and ruin. While many wish to produce a narrative of historical events from archaeological remains, archaeology's temporality, as a form of memory practice, is one of *articulation,* of relation between past and present through duration and material persistence; this is the *actuality* of the past. Historiography, in contrast, typically seeks descriptive or analytic narratives or models of the flow of historical events tied to dates and a linear notion of time, and is focused principally upon the past, rather than the past-in-the-present.

Consider then the implication of this temporality of actuality in relation to risk society. The paradox or contradiction is that the control that systematic knowledge affords, for example, in managing the erosive impact of development or of the trade in illicit antiquities on the possibility of a past in the future, comes at the cost of a sense of security. It is not just that the past (in the present) is threatened; senses of personal and community identity are threatened, when the continuity of the past is the source of such identity. The growth of these systems of calculation and control is intimately connected with growing political, social, cultural and indeed *ontological* insecurity.

What I mean by this is that the security threat which individuals face is, at base, a threat to their very identity because of the ways in which these abstract systems of knowledge work. When who you are, including your history, is no longer given by traditional institutions and cultures, but is constantly at risk, if who and what you are is subject to changing expert research, or to loss of employment, the challenge to individuals is to constantly construct and reconstruct their own identity. The growing absence of traditional sources of authority, a durable and persistent past, in answering who we are accompanies a growing emphasis upon individuals to take responsibility for self and decisions, to monitor self, to self-reflect and to assert their own agency, exercise discipline in being who they are. This responsibility is, of course, full of risk. You might not get it right. You might not even be able to create a coherent and secure sense of self identity, not least because you may not have the resources: the possibility of asserting individual agency is seriously circumscribed by horizontal and vertical divisions in society, by class, gender and ethnicity.

This is a rough sketch of the contemporary setting within which the archaeological imagination works upon ruins and remains. I am now going to outline how I intend to delve into the details of this relationship between modernity and the material past-in-the-present, for I suggest that it is in the investigation of particular manifestations of the archaeological imagination in its modern infancy that we will achieve the best understanding.

1.3 *The Form of this Book*

If, as I have remarked, we are all antiquarians and archaeologists now, and if I wish to take up detailed case studies, in order to achieve analytical insight, where do I begin? For several years in my blog (at *mshanks.com*) I have plunged *in medias res,* with a running commentary on encounters with the archaeological imagination (among other topics). The list of entries is very diverse, covering ongoing debates about archaeological discoveries, news about digital media (many matters of archive and memory are being worked out in new media), particular exhibitions and pieces of contemporary art, as well as ruminations on everyday happenings in the life of an academic in Silicon Valley. While I have tried to be analytical, the collection is not immediately coherent as an *account*: the archaeological imagination is difficult to contain, as an emergent feature of an ecology of practices so dispersed through modernity.

When I first conceived this book I considered offering a set of themes and some examples of each. But again, which examples? To follow the genealogical and symptomatic approach just outlined, I have chosen instead to focus on the manifestations of the archaeological imagination in one region's own history, community and material heritage. I present nine sets of scenarios or micro narratives involving antiquarians in the eighteenth and nineteenth centuries associated with the Borders between England and Scotland. It was a remarkable region then, a core of modern industrial reason and enlightenment as well as a long-standing buffer zone between the old monarchies and nation states of England and Scotland. For some years now I have been pursuing my own archaeological project investigating the long term history of the Borders, especially through fieldwork and survey centered upon the Roman town of Binchester (also to be found at *Vinovium.org*), so I am able to make connections across the kinds of different social and cultural fields brought together in an archaeological sensibility. Margins and edges are, after all, so often where things become clear: I will treat the Borders as a lens through which to focus the archaeological imagination. The Borders in the emerging modernity of the long eighteenth century could even be called a microcosm of the archaeological imagination.

This book is an essay in the sense of a trial—trying out ideas, working on some in detail to see if they offer sustainable insights. This is a *personal* trial, offering an inflected perspective, on the argument that a key component of archaeological ways of thinking is indeed personal standpoint, in a context of sometimes considerable *state* investment in heritage and stewardship of the remains of the past. My standpoint is the one just mentioned: my own project of a regional chorography of the Borders (as I will define the term in the course of the book). I offer the scenarios and stories of the Borders as *cultural probes,* a term coined by Marshall McLuhan to refer to pointed insertions or interventions that reveal symptomatic responses through which a condition or state of being may be assessed. Do something, create an event, a happening, and watch what ensues—it can be very revealing of underlying structure. Blunt probes are less effective than those sharp and targeted. Best insight comes from careful and precise dissection. So my nine scenarios are rather detailed. Here I ask the reader's indulgence. Sometimes a line of narrative and reasoning may appear puzzling, given the ostensible topic of the archaeological imagination. I have planned these to be only temporary mysteries (and I admit to being influenced by James Burke's extraordinary revelations of the logic sometimes to be found behind apparently disconnected historical events and persons: see, for example, *Circles:Fifty Roundtrips Through History, Technology, Science, Culture* [Burke 2000]). I also propose that if we do wish to understand, for example, the way nationalist ideology informs archaeological work, we need precise and local dissection of particular practices; this is what will be found in the scenarios. Nevertheless, to help maintain orientation, I provide a running commentary that connects the eighteenth century stories with our contemporary experiences of the archaeological imagination.

This commentary prefigures analysis. The stories are followed by some graphics, diagrams that offer a kind of navigation through the archaeological imagination; I also offer a breakdown of topics and emblems in a *narratology* inspired by the semiotician Greimas (particularly Greimas and Fontanille 1993): digging into the grammar of the archaeological imagination. The analysis, stories and diagrams are but entry points into what is an indeterminate field, with great cascades of connections. To help further exploration there is a Website to accompany this book, at *archaeopaedia.com.* There can be found a glossary, bibliography, and many more examples and illustrations; it is interactive and open to edit, which means that anyone may contribute stories, images, or remarks.

The Borders offer an encounter between different mentalities or individual applications of an archaeological imagination. The novelist Walter Scott is one who dominates these stories, because his work so embodies the tensions and contradictions that preceded the consolidation of the discipline of archaeology in the mid nineteenth century. I will present him in many debates with other antiquarian interests and positions. In the shadows, and not so much the subject of the book per se, is the twentieth century critic Walter Benjamin, with his own version of the archaeological imagination rooted in actuality, the non-arbitrary conjuncture of past and present, in a society marked by crisis and the decline of tradition (the subject of Laurent Olivier's work, *Le Sombre Abîme du Temps* [2008], cited above).

Before I move to the Borders, I need to clarify a point I wish to make about the way an archaeological sensibility connects with systematic knowledge and archaeological science; the way art, systematic knowledge and science connect in the cultural imaginary.

1.4 *An Argument about Science and Enlightenment*

The notion of an archaeological imagination takes us far beyond the academic discipline and profession. An argument of this book, more implicit than carefully laid out, concerns the history of disciplines like archaeology. Most accounts, going back beyond Glyn Daniel's fine pioneering book *A Hundred Years of Archeology*, published in 1950, tell the story of archaeology as one of breakthroughs, discoveries sometimes, watersheds in archaeological thinking established by the great exponents and typically centered upon archaeological sites and finds. Some correct the details, others offer contextual accounts, providing social and cultural context (I have already mentioned Bruce Trigger's socially deterministic history of archaeological thought), even revisionist correction, displaying the importance of gender and cultural politics, for example, in shaping the discipline. But there is a clear orthodoxy and conventional narrative: it is one of the triumph of reason. Archaeology was a (late-born) child of Enlightenment reason, the story goes, deeply connected with geological and evolutionary accounts of human origins, and was part of the struggle against pre-modern superstition and dogma. Such an account helps make us think we are modern, that we have come some great way in our scientific endeavors of the last two hundred years, and are different from, better than our forebears who were perhaps fascinated by similar things, but practiced something that was antiquarianism at best, and certainly wasn't modern archaeology. People once even thought, and not that long ago, that ancient stone tools were thunderbolts!

I really don't want to make such judgments. When I actually read eighteenth century antiquarians, I am always wonderfully surprised at their sophistication. Stuart Piggott, one of the first archaeologists to take the antiquarian history of his discipline seriously, insisted that from the early eighteenth century antiquarian study of the material past became suffused with superstition and flimsy nonsense, epitomized by the contradiction, as Piggott sees it, in the life work of antiquarian William Stukeley—between his fine fieldwork skills, exemplified in his accurate field surveys, and his obsession with Druids, part of his supposedly naive and mythographic account of British history. The march of reason faltered, temporarily, we are told, and regained strength and stability when the antiquarian became the archaeologist. I wish to resist this anachronistic tendency to judge the past according to our own supposedly superior standards.

This is a crucial subtext of this book: to understand a discipline like archaeology, do not start with its own self-definition, but with practices that have come to be called archaeological. This is why this book is about something more than the discipline: its topic is an aptitude, sensibility, faculty, a disposition underlying cognate and disparate practices and procedures, the *work* of the archaeological imagination, now associated with archaeology, anthropology and history. When we consider what people do and think about the past, the way they document and illustrate memories, ruins and remains, processing sources, making forays and interventions in land and property, publishing and sharing their findings, I suggest that it becomes clear that archaeology is but one standardized mode of engagement with the past and with material remains and sources, or rather it is one set of relationships, albeit now comparatively well-resourced and certainly authorized and sanctioned by State and Academy. Part of this *symptomatic* focus on particular practices, rather than the ways they are categorized and valued, is to deny the radical separation of disciplines that is still so characteristic of scholarship and the academy today. As I will show, albeit in a small way, hard and empirical rationalism accompanied a celebration of poetic and speculative elaboration in antiquarian scholarship; we lose too much in radically separating research and the imaginary. The archaeological *imagination* has always been at the heart of archaeological *science*.

A strong case can be made, I believe, that the antiquarian of the eighteenth century was not marginalized and replaced by the practitioner of archaeological science. The conundrums and contradictions of antiquarianism are very much alive with us. Antiquarianism has been massively successful, I would argue; we just don't call it by that name any more. It is possible to hold that my topic is not the archaeological, but the *antiquarian* imagination. It is an antiquarian imagination, part art, part science, widely embodied in experimental natural philosophy, exemplifying a critical romanticism, that was institutionalized in state museums and then in the academy, where it became archaeology, while also lending cultural force to burgeoning experiences of travel, tourism, heritage and a gamut of charged relationships between past and present. I am fond of saying that we are all archaeologists today, somewhat obsessed with the remains of the past in the present. I might more accurately say that today we are all antiquarians!

2. Debatable Lands

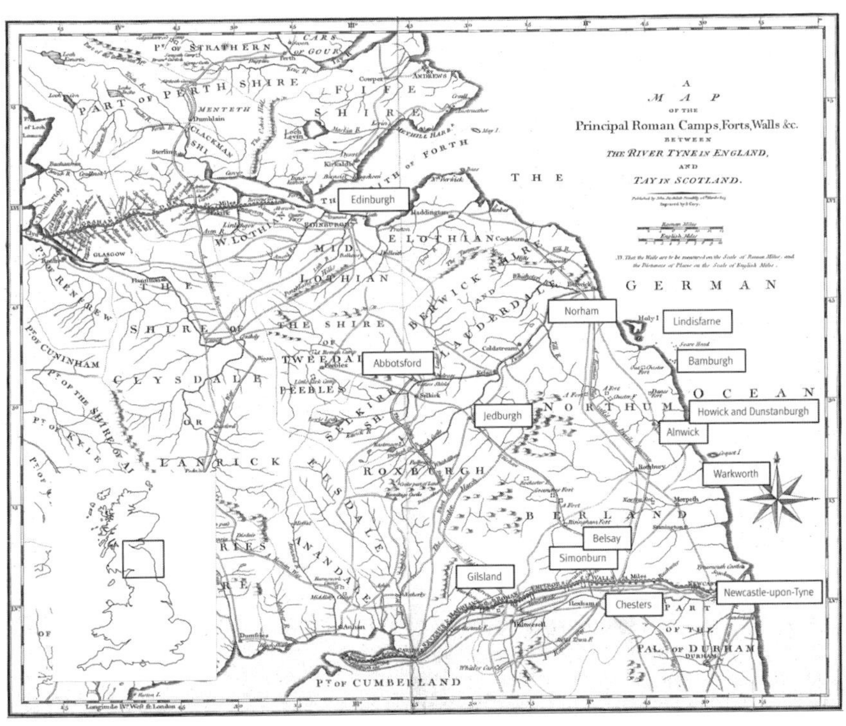

Map of the Borderlands between England and Scotland.

Chapter Two

2.1 *A Northern Stage*

My proposition is that what I have defined as our contemporary archaeological imagination has deep genealogical roots in the political changes of the seventeenth and eighteenth centuries in northern and western Europe, in the Age of Reason, with experimental method and the formation of modern disciplinary science and learning, challenges to absolutist monarchy, with modern nationalism and the nation state. I am going to explore this world of the antiquarian as a way of unraveling the components of an archaeological sensibility.

But I am not aiming to deliver another history of archaeology based on such broad themes; my account will involve far more than holding that archaeology begins with antiquarian interests in collection and antiquities. Let me take us back to the borders between England and Scotland, between the Rivers Tyne and Tweed in Northumberland, north of Hadrian's Wall, a land of Scottish Enlightenment and English Industrial Revolution. In this chapter I am going to set the scene for the ramble of scenarios at the heart of this essay.

The contemporary line on the map is almost incidental, because the Borders between Scotland and England are a distinct and continuous, though heterogeneous, region, ranging between uplands and lowlands. Neither the north of England nor the lowlands of Scotland geographically stop at the current political border. It is a landscape with few large towns between Edinburgh, Carlisle in the west and Newcastle in the east. With the Southern Uplands of Dumfries and Galloway included to the west, the border region, comprising the counties of Northumberland, Durham, and Cumbria, and the county now called The Scottish Borders, covers about 10,000 square miles of rolling hills and sometimes quite remote valleys, even today, and with few easy routes cutting across the whole region.

This rich archaeological landscape has conspicuous remains of prosperous early farming, especially on the lighter soils of the

---

The Archaeological Imagination by Michael Shanks, 43–126.

Millfield basin in the north of Northumberland, and even a coastal mesolithic hamlet, at Howick, one of the best preserved in Europe; prehistoric rock art is an outstanding feature in the east, and there is clear cultural continuity through the many hillforts of later prehistory. Roman authors do distinguish distinct tribal groups, and it is with Roman colonial occupation that the region becomes a political buffer zone between the province of Britannia and the people to the north, called, among many other names, *Caledonii*. In the second century the Emperor Hadrian authorized the building of one of the greatest engineering works of antiquity, the wall across the country that now bears his name and marked the limits of Roman rule.

The Kingdom of Northumbria, centered on the lowland east of the region, followed secession from the Roman Empire, and early Celtic Christian culture, the world of the Venerable Bede, Saints Aidan, Oswald and Cuthbert, was conspicuously vigorous and accomplished. But from the thirteenth century, in the wake of Edward Longshanks's claim on the Scottish throne, the region became again a buffer zone, this time between the kingdoms of Scotland and England. Known as the Middle Marches, it bore the brunt of intermittent warfare for three hundred years, and was subject to constant raiding and internecine conflict. Remains of these times are everywhere—great fortresses such as Alnwick of the Percy family, Roxburgh, Bamburgh on the coast, and many hundreds of fortified houses, pele towers and bastles, as they are known locally.

Refortification of the border, of Hadrian's Wall, was considered in the sixteenth century reign of Elizabeth I, but the union of the crowns of Scotland and England under the Stewarts in the seventeenth century began a process of pacification of the Borders. It was not easy. The remote upland valleys such as Tynedale, Redesdale and Liddesdale showed distinct similarities to the world of the Highland Scottish clans further north and were removed from any kind of state control, dominated by clan chiefs and family ties. Part of the Borders was officially known as "The Debatable Lands" in reference to this independence and lawlessness. This was the land of the raiding *Border Reiver and Mosstrooper.*

Political authority in Scotland passed from Edinburgh to Parliament in London at the beginning of the eighteenth century. Religious and political differences, notably centered upon Catholicism and various Anglican and Protestant sects, had long affected the region and lay behind the challenges to the throne in the rebellions of 1715 and 1745, the latter involving the Young Pretender, Charles Edward Stuart, Bonnie Prince Charlie. These failed challenges to the Hanoverian monarchy in England had enormous political and cultural consequences, leading to a state clampdown on the Highland clans and investment, through military works, in an infrastructure of roads, not seen since Roman times, intended to open up the landscape. The region was also mapped comprehensively, a cartographic project later extended in the institution of the Ordnance Survey, the first major state-sponsored project of coherent spatial documentation dedicated to property and control.

Edinburgh, in spite of, or perhaps because of, the removal of political power, and with one of the first public education systems in western Europe since Roman times, went from a small urban backwater in the early eighteenth century to become one of the intellectual centers of Enlightenment Europe. New humanist and rationalist thinking in moral and political philosophy, political economy, medicine, geology, history and literature, was pioneered by the likes of David Hume, Adam Smith, Adam Ferguson, Robert Burns, James Hutton and Walter Scott. Their work remains current and pertinent today. Neo-liberal political ideologies, since Thatcher's and Reagan's championship of the ideas of the likes of Milton Friedman and Friedrich Hayek in the 1970s, continue in active engagement with the political economy of Adam Smith and others in the Scottish Enlightenment. Constitutional theory remains similarly indebted to eighteenth century Scottish thought.

Discussion and debate was centered upon a public sphere of cafés and meetinghouses as well as the university. Benefiting from the buoyant economy of a growing British Empire, Edinburgh embarked on a radical program of urban development from 1765, with its startling neo-Classical New Town offering considerable improvement to the overcrowded old city.

Urban development to the south, in Newcastle-upon-Tyne, came later, from the 1820s, with a comparable program of urban planning in neo-Classical style, known locally as Grainger Town, after the principal architect. Here the impetus was industrialization. By the second quarter of the nineteenth century, Newcastle upon Tyne and its conurbation was the center of heavy manufacturing, chemical and extractive industries rooted in a long history of mining, trade and manufacture. Innovation was a cornerstone of regional development; Newcastle-upon-Tyne was the Silicon Valley of its day.

Hard-headed business interest combined with intellectual speculation, philosophy and literary pursuits with technological innovation, design and agricultural improvement across the networks of association and discussion between Scottish Enlightenment and English industrialization. The *Society for the Improvement of Medical Knowledge* (1731) became the *Edinburgh Society for Improving Arts and Sciences and particularly Natural Knowledge* and then the *Royal Society of Edinburgh* in 1783. The *Literary and Philosophical Society of Newcastle* was founded in 1793 as a forum for new ideas in any field. Antiquarian pursuits and interests were far from incidental. Both *The Society of Antiquaries of Scotland* and *The Society of Antiquaries of Newcastle upon Tyne* were early foundations in 1780 and 1813; both were keenly supported by all manner of businessmen, developers, speculators, and intellectuals.

So this is the setting for my collection of short scenarios. Let me start by zooming in on a footnote in an old guide to Border ruins. Remember the spirit of my exploration—insight is to be found in details, in the working of cultural and historical structures through the micro-articulations effected in what people get up to.

2.2 *Relics and Witnesses*

Walter Scott was an antiquarian, musicologist, novelist, essayist, collector, landowner, part-time militiaman, magistrate, poet, and bestselling author in the book trade of the early nineteenth century. His home and world, the setting for most of his life and writing, was the borderland between Scotland and England, between the Scottish lowlands and Highlands, and between past and present. His *Border Antiquities of England and Scotland* was published in 1814. The two volumes, profusely and wonderfully illustrated with engravings, are subtitled *Comprising Specimens of Architecture and Sculpture, and other vestiges of former ages, accompanied by descriptions. Together with Illustrations of remarkable incidents in Border History and tradition, and Original Poetry.* The work is a gazetteer of archaeological and antiquarian interests.

A long introduction takes the reader through a historical narrative of the borders. On pages xviii–xix Scott is dealing with the extensive archaeological remains of Hadrian's Wall, that seventy mile long feat of Roman engineering that had marked the edge of empire, separating the province of Britannia from the north. He wrote: "The most entire part of this celebrated monument, which is now, owing to the progress of improvement and enclosure, subjected to constant dilapidation, is to be found at a place called Glenwhelt, in the neighbourhood of Gilsland Spaw."

In a footnote Scott takes us back thirteen years to his cottage in Lasswade, just south of Edinburgh. James Hogg, the "Ettrick Shepherd," dined with him there (and this is a whole other remarkable story), as did the Wordsworths. In 1801, on the occasion of a visit from the literary antiquarian Joseph Ritson:

> The wall was mentioned; and Mr. Ritson, who had been misinformed by some ignorant person at Hexham, was disposed strongly to dispute that any reliques of it yet remained. The author mentioned the place in the text (Glenwhelt), and said that there was as much of it standing as would break the neck of Mr. Ritson's informer were he to fall from it. Of this careless and metaphorical expression Mr. Ritson failed not to make a memorandum, and afterwards wrote to

> the author, that he had visited the place with the express purpose of jumping down from the wall in order to confute what he supposed a hyperbole. But he added, that, though not yet satisfied that it was quite high enough to break a man's neck, it was of elevation sufficient to render the experiment very dangerous. (Scott 1814, xviii)

A pleasant anecdote and quite straightforward, it might seem: Ritson was simply interested enough in the Roman Wall to see whether there were indeed surviving remains. Actually, the anecdote doesn't make sense in these terms; it is far more revealing.

It is very unlikely that Ritson, a noted and notoriously informed antiquarian, hadn't read the many accounts of the Wall published since the sixteenth century. Alexander Gordon had produced a fastidious report of an encounter with the Roman remains in his *Itinerarium Septentrionale* of 1726. In its wake in 1732 came *Britannia Romana*, the classic account of Roman Britain by John Horsley, a native of Northumberland and local cleric. It contained a fine set of maps based on a new survey by George Mark. The Wall was well documented.

How could Hadrian's Wall have been so little known to Ritson? Born in 1752, he was raised in Stockton, County Durham, just to the south of the Wall, and practiced law there before moving to London to become a core member of the antiquarian community. Were archaeological interests in ancient monuments themselves so little shared that he could doubt that anything was left? The central sections of the Wall had been difficult of access only seventy or so years previous, but that had changed since the building of the Military Road along the course of the Wall in the 1750s. General Wade directed the project according to an Act of Parliament to facilitate the passage of troops across the country from Carlisle to Newcastle; the road was part of an extensive program designed to open up the northern and Scottish landscapes that had favored the recent Scottish rebellions of 1715 and 1745. To keep costs down the Military Road made much use of Roman stone, and its route, frequently on top of the Roman monument itself, was chosen more to avoid damage to surrounding agricultural land than out of respect for antiquity. Perhaps Ritson knew very well of this

Figure 1 Hadrian's Wall, Walltown Crags, east of Gilsland, 2010.

destruction of the monument and this was the reason for his visit to Glenwhelt, to see how much was actually left. If so, why was he relating evidence from a local of the town of Hexham?

There may be a clue to the significance of the anecdote in Scott's language. Ritson disputes that any "reliques" of the Wall yet remained. By the time Scott was writing the *Border Antiquities* in 1814 "reliques" was an archaic spelling (Scott uses the spelling again, significantly, in his novel of 1816, *The Antiquary*, discussed below). He is almost certainly making reference to a famous work by Bishop Thomas Percy, his *Reliques of Ancient English Poetry* (many editions from 1765), because Ritson had entered into a public argument with Percy over the collection. Let me elaborate.

Ritson's reputation still stands on an exhaustive study of "the historical or poetic remains" of the legend of Robin Hood (*Robin Hood: a collection of all the ancient poems, songs, and ballads now extant, relative to that celebrated English outlaw*, first published in 1795). In 1800 he worked with Scott on a scholarly edition of ancient border ballads (published under Scott's name as *Minstrelsy of the Scottish Border*). In his day he was renowned for his philological accuracy and obsession with establishing the authenticity of manuscript sources. His reputation, however, was also one of a sour critic, and he was involved in some vitriolic debates about literary scholarship and what he claimed were modern forgeries of ancient manuscripts and sources.

It had begun in 1782 when Ritson published a fifty-page pamphlet entitled *Observations on the Three First Volumes of the 'History of English Poetry,'* a vicious attack on the work of Thomas Warton, a well-respected and well-liked literary scholar and antiquary. Ritson accused Warton of ignorance, plagiarism, and every sort of literary fraud. Further criticism followed of editions of Shakespeare (including Samuel Johnson's of 1778), all of which accompanied publication of his own editions of ancient poetry. His *Select Collection of English Songs* appeared in 1783. The preface on the origin and progress of national song featured a vehement attack on Percy's *Reliques*. The full title of this collection was *Reliques of Ancient English Poetry: consisting of old heroic ballads, songs, and other pieces of our earlier poets. (Chiefly of the lyric kind). Together with some few of later date*. It purported to be a historical collection based upon various manuscript and oral sources, and with an element of the modern. Ritson admitted that Percy's work had merit, but he also accused him of having included forged or garbled versions of many ballads. In 1791 Ritson published *Pieces of Ancient Popular Poetry from Authentic Manuscripts and Old Printed Copies*, and he followed that the next year with *Ancient Songs from the Time of King Henry the Third to the Revolution*. The prefatory essays again pursued Percy by throwing doubt on the existence of his main manuscript, the "reliques" from which he claimed to have derived his ballads.

It was this attitude, what Scott calls a "zeal for accuracy," that may have meant that Ritson had to get out in the field and witness the Wall itself in order to check what he had been *told* by the "ignorant person in Hexham" as well as Scott, and to authenticate the *written* accounts of the *remains* from the likes of Gordon and Horsley. I have highlighted *told* and *written* and *remains*, because I think there is more to Ritson's mistrust than just mild inquisitiveness: I suggest that at its heart is the matter of authenticity and the figure of the witness, the very subjects of history. Ritson needed to *connect* the different accounts with the artifact itself, the Wall.

Antiquarian interest from the sixteenth century focused upon collecting old things and encountering ancient monuments in the landscape. Throughout the eighteenth century antiquarians and what we would now call ethnomusicologists were collecting oral and textual sources for medieval and earlier literature and song, delving into dim stretches of European history. Scott, Ritson and Percy were major figures in this effort. The most famous and controversial perhaps was James Macpherson who translated and published from 1762 what he claimed to be the lost work of the ancient Gaelic Bard Ossian.

Fakes abounded, and it was often difficult to distinguish authenticity; Macpherson was widely criticized and almost certainly wrote a lot, even most, of Ossian himself. A favorite case of mine appears in William Hutchinson's *View of Northumberland* of 1778. In Volume II of this sound scholarly exposition of local antiquities and history, Hutchinson records, on pages 162–164, the discovery by the local Vicar of Norham, a village in the north of the county on the river Tweed, of an ancient transcription of a ballad by a thirteenth century Cheviot hill shepherd called Duncan Frasier. *The Laidley Worm of Spindleston Heughs* is a classic fairy-tale romance set at the royal court of Bamburgh in the ancient kingdom of Northumbria. The poem is about a witch, a princess-turned-dragon, and a heroic Saxon knight, Childy Wynds, who encounters the beast that lays waste to the land and rescues the princess through a kiss that turns her back to human form. Even now you may visit the site of the magical transformation and triumph of love. As direct result of Hutchinson's county history, the state-authorized maps of the Ordnance Survey, instituted in 1790 following the pioneering mapping of the Highlands under "Butcher" Cumberland after the '45 Jacobite rising, mark the location of the "Trough of the Laidley Worm" under the heugh (a rock edge), where the worm, the dragon, drank. And indeed there is a damp hollow by the modern trailer park; my daughter and son, Molly and Ben, were much taken by it when we visited in 2008.

Later, however, it became clear, as reported in a local biographical work, *Men of Mark Twixt Tyne and Tees* (Richard Welford, 1895, Volume III, 4–5), that the Vicar of Norham, John Lamb, was quite a practical joker, albeit a learned one. The ballad reads quite obviously as eighteenth century pastiche, with Lamb, having written the ballad himself, poking gentle fun at antiquarian concerns with dim heroic pasts, in the same way that Scott mocks Jonathan Oldbuck, the character of the antiquary in his gothic novel of the same name (see below).

Hutchinson was completely taken in because the line between original, restoration and fake was not absolute. How could it be? Ruins and relics are broken and incomplete by definition; they *require* conservation, care, restoration, amendment, the *work* of the antiquarian. What could be authentic origin or historical source? Only, ultimately, the *voice* of the past. Hutchinson, courtesy of the Vicar of Norham, could name the voice, the shepherd Duncan Frasier, in the border uplands that had harbored ancient clan society within the reach of living memory. Many antiquarians quite freely adapted and restored old works alongside their own writing. Percy was generous in his editing of sources, improving them where he thought fit. Scott's edition of ancient border ballads (the *Minstrelsy*) on which Ritson had worked similarly took a heavy hand in editing ancient originals; Scott added his own poetry to his *Border Antiquities*.

The search was on for authentic origins. Percy's collection was significantly titled *Reliques of Ancient* English *Poetry*. Macpherson, in contrast, was resurrecting Gaelic and Irish ghosts. The voices of minstrels and bards echo from times when the epic poem reflected feudal order, represented by the poet as a performing subject in the service of social betters. Alexander Gordon's project, enacted in his journey south, the *Itinerarium*, was to encounter and document Roman remains and establish a particular relationship between Scotland and England, the vitality of barbarian indigeneity versus classical civility; he came down firmly on the side of the former. Roman remains were the border of this distinction, the issue being whether Hadrian's Wall marked the edge of civilization, or whether it was built to keep at bay the strength of Caledonian culture, a Scottish, "barbarian" alternative. Roman Wall or Pict's Wall? Richard Hingley has well explored these tensions in his 2008 book *Recovery of Roman Britain 1586–1906*.

Ritson's doubts about what he had been told of the Roman Wall are thus symptomatic of contemporary anxieties about the ways that the past informs the present, and in this there are questions of the role of the author, editor, and scholar. Who is speaking for whom? What is the relationship of representation between voice, text and author? In all his work Ritson approaches the questions through the more formal aspects of source criticism; he rigorously read for consistency of language, seeking signs of stylistic deviation from what would be expected of a text given date, provenance and provenience. These, for Ritson, are the matters of historical sources. He applied careful scrutiny backed by reason. His Jacobin support of the French Revolution is no surprise, on this account, because it was a cause of reasoned, *rational* political rule; others, as I will discuss in following sections, make reference to much wider issues of taste, identity, property and ownership.

Scott and Ritson plunge us into a nexus of issues and anxieties surrounding heritage and identity. I suggest that what I have just presented is the way that national identities were and still are worked out through much wider debates about accuracy, authority, authenticity, insider and outsider, local and expert, and ancient ancestries embodied in text and artifact. Who is speaking for whom, and on what basis? What does it mean to be an indigenous native? How does this matter of voice and (political) representation relate to "globalist" forces such as the Roman Catholic Church, to imperialist ambitions of the likes of the Roman and British empires? Deeply implicated are questions of record and witnessing, legal and ethical matters—who and what do you believe? Here in the United States we have had several decades of contention over the relative status of archaeological accounts and Native American traditions. The force of indigenous rights to knowledge and cultural property is the core of the agenda of the *World Archaeological Congress*.

The relationships with European Romanticism are clear. Here we are at a Celtic fringe, where English and Scottish blur, where ancient voices are excavated, dragged from oblivion and shared in an international European cultural sphere of reasoned debate about history and historiography. The task—to bring the very landscape to bear upon definitions of ancestry and identity. Who you are and where you come from—though these may not be as transparent as you might think.

And consider the prominence of the figure of the *witness* in these scenarios. Let me shift register to contemporary popular culture. The *X-Files* (screenwriter, Chris Carter) has been one of the most popular science fiction series on American TV, running originally from 1993 to 2002. Fox Mulder and Dana Scully are a detective duo investigating paranormal activity: one is a believer, the other a critical skeptic. The show tapped into tensions and anxieties around government and corporate interference in evidence, conspiracy theories and cover-ups. This thematic was expressed in slogans such as "trust no one" and "the truth is out there"—go seek the evidence, though you may have to rely on hearsay, because the evidence is deliberately obscured. Here again is that contrast between (sound) evidence and (authentic) voice.

2.3 *Durat Opus Vatum*

The frontispiece to the first 1765 edition of Thomas Percy's *Reliques of Ancient English Poetry* shows a bard or minstrel playing his lyre and reciting poetry to a small audience of medieval ladies and lords, two in armor, in a parkland landscape in front of a castle. Above in the clouds a cherub showers down flowers from a basket while two others carry a banner with a motto "NON OMNIS MORIAR"—I will not entirely die. This is from a poem by the Roman Horace (*Carmina* 3.30) where he claims his poetry is a monument more durable than bronze, higher than an Egyptian pyramid, reaching back into the depths of history, and, even though he is of lowly birth, as a poet he will be spoken of for eternity. On the facing title page is an emblem of a lyre propped against a blasted dead tree in a medieval ruin; in front a book and manuscript pages are scattered above the motto "DURAT OPUS VATUM"—the work of poets endures, a sentiment found in the Third Book of Ovid's *Amores,* in Elegy IX which commemorates the death of the Roman poet Tibullus. The Roman *vates* is the poet who speaks from the inspiration of the divine muses and so transcends time, even prophetically seeing into the future; the creativity of the prophet-poet bridges past, present and future; his work even escapes death. In contrast, stone buildings fall into ruin and writings are scattered to the wind. But Percy's is not a collection of classical poets, and the inspiration is not from Apollo. This is an *English* milieu of the eighteenth century, set in the borders with Scotland.

Here, captured in an allegorical iconography, is that contrast I have been discussing between living voice and history's ruin, between presence and loss: the character of history's sources implicated in the very identity of a people and its future. Another theme is that of material connection between past and present, the transmission of family and memory. What endures? How can time be crossed? How can we reach back in time, project forward? Time travel.

It was while visiting a colleague in 1753 that Thomas Percy had noticed a battered volume "lying dirty on the floor, under a bureau in the parlour ... being used by the maids to light the fire" (quoted by

Figure 2 *Durat Opus Vatum*. Appearing on the Title Page of Thomas Percy, *Reliques of Ancient English Poetry,* 1765.

Palmer 2004). This proved to be a seventeenth-century folio manuscript, a collection of poems and ballads. It was to be the basis for his own anthology. By 1765 he had completed his editing and was chaplain and secretary to the Earl (later Duke) of Northumberland and tutor to his son, Algernon. The *Reliques* is dedicated to the Countess of Northumberland, who, as Baroness Percy, shared the ancient and illustrious northern name of Percy:

> By such Bards, Madam, as I am now introducing to your presence, was the infancy of genius nurtured and advanced … by such were the heroic deeds of the Earls of Northumberland sung at festivals in the Hall of Alnwick: and those songs, which the bounty of your ancestors rewarded, now return to your Ladyship by a kind of hereditary right. (Percy 1765, Dedication.)

The new Duke and Duchess of Northumberland were prominent members of the aristocracy, living at Syon House in west London, with its 200 acre park; at Northumberland House, by what is now Trafalgar Square; and in Northumberland at the ancient castle of Alnwick. The dedication page bears an illustration of another northern Percy stronghold, Warkworth Castle, with its unique and massive keep featured behind a heraldic coat of arms.

The stress placed on ancestry by Percy in the dedication is ironically appropriate. Yes, these ballads reach back to feudal times, and the Percys were indeed the most powerful and wealthy family of northern nobility on the English side of the border. Their name appears in many of the ballads; Thomas Percy hastened the publication of a third volume of *Reliques* to include more that mentioned the family. The Percys had a checkered history, falling in and out of favor with various English and Scottish monarchs, and were featured as such in several of Shakespeare's plays. Though recreated several times, the Earldom of Northumberland was mostly associated with the Percy family. They had arrived in England with William of Normandy in 1066, but the male line had become extinct in 1670. The last Earl of Northumberland's heiress married the sixth Duke of Somerset—the "Proud Duke" (he was so inflated with rank and genealogy that he insisted that his children always stand in his presence, disinheriting a daughter whom he discovered to have sat while he napped). In 1740 the Proud Duke's granddaughter married Sir Hugh Smithson, a Yorkshire baronet whose family had been ennobled in 1660 on the basis of money they made in their haberdasher's shop in Cheapside, London. Four years later her brother's unexpected death made Elizabeth Seymour, as she then was, a great heiress. In 1749 the ancient Northumberland Earldom was revived for her father, with a special provision that it passed on his death (in 1750) to Smithson, who took the name of Percy. The new Duke and Duchess could be expected therefore to be somewhat sensitive about their ancestral claims. Later I will take up their Gothic restoration of Alnwick castle; here I want to pursue this topic of the poet's voice.

Percy's was a work of antiquarian rescue, the compilation of ballads and poems, apparently transcribed from their oral originals, depicting a medieval world of heroic encounters, recalled in the bard or minstrel's performances in the halls of clan chiefs. Three years before the publication of Percy's *English* collection, Macpherson had released the first examples of what he claimed to be a remarkable discovery—the lost works of a Gaelic epic poet, Ossian, who sang of a lost golden age of Scottish history. The poems achieved international success. Napoleon and Thomas Jefferson were great admirers. Goethe admired, translated and incorporated Ossian into his own work (*The Sorrows of Young Werther*). Schubert set Ossian to music. Across Europe the poems were proclaimed as a Celtic equivalent of Classical writers such as Homer—Ossian was the Homer of the north.

Ossian is not now often read or quoted, but attention to the work offers insight into this popularity and effect, and to the character of its "archaeology." Mention must be made of the persistent theme of the voice of the bard echoing through the Scottish Highlands, of constant auditory metaphor and imagery. Here is the beginning of *Conlath and Cuthóna: a Poem* (Volume 1, page 171 in the third edition of 1765):

> Did not Ossian hear a voice? or is it the sound of days that are no more? Often does the memory of former times come, like the evening sun, on my soul. The noise of the chace is renewed, and, in thought, I lift the spear.—But Ossian did hear a voice: Who art thou, son of the night? The sons of little men are asleep, and the midnight wind is in my hall. Perhaps it is the shield of Fingal that echoes to the blast, it hangs in Ossian's hall, and he feels it sometimes with his hands.—Yes!—I hear thee, my friend: long has thy voice been absent from my ear! What brings thee, on thy cloud, to Ossian, son of the generous Morni? Are the friends of the aged near thee? Where is Oscar, son of fame?—He was often near thee, O Conlath, when the din of battle rose.
>
> *Ghost of Conlath*
>
> *Sleeps the sweet voice of Cona, in the midst of his rustling hall?*
> *Sleeps Ossian in his hall, and his friends without their fame?*
> *The sea rolls around the dark I-thona, and our tombs are not seen*
> *by the stranger.*
> *How long shall our fame be unheard, son of the echoing Morven?*

Macpherson introduces the poem as follows:

> Conlath was the youngest of Morni's sons, and brother to the celebrated Gaul, who is so often mentioned in Ossian's poems. He was in love with Cuthóna, the daughter of Rumar, when Toscar the son of Kinfena, accompanied by Fercuth his friend, arrived, from Ireland, at Mora where Conlath dwelt. He was hospitably received, and according to the custom of the times feasted, three days, with Conlath. On the fourth he set sail, and coasting the island of waves, probably, one of the Hebrides, he saw Cuthóna hunting, fell in love with her, and carried her away, by force, in his ship. He was forced, by stress of weather, into I-thona, a desert isle. In the mean time Conlath, hearing of the rape, sailed after him, and found him on the point of sailing for the coast of Ireland. They fought; and they, and their followers fell by mutual wounds. Cuthóna did not long survive: for she died of grief the third day after. Fingal, hearing of their unfortunate death, sent Stormal the son of Moran to bury them, but forgot to send a bard to sing the funeral song over their tombs. The ghost of Conlath came, long after, to Ossian, to intreat him to transmit, to posterity, his and Cuthóna's fame. For it was the opinion of the times, that the souls of the deceased were not happy, till their elegies were composed by a bard.—Thus is the story of the poem handed down by tradition.

The authenticity of Percy's and Macpherson's collections was doubted and debated from the outset, as I have indicated already. The argument was not so much against the restoration of old poetry; it concerned the authenticity of the national tradition and character represented by the body of work, and the artistry and taste of the restorations. The topic was the role of the scholar in editing text, and, more crucially, the role of the scholar in witnessing and representing local oral tradition and performance, the deep-rooted indigenous practices of a regional or national community, as evidenced in different kinds of sources. The arguments were about voice and memory, descent, tradition and genealogy. For there were actual manuscripts and transcriptions. When Percy's battered folio was made public in 1867 (it is now in the British Library), Ritson's criticisms seemed justified, that the "learned collector has preferred his ingenuity to his fidelity," that Percy printed scarcely "a single poem ... fairly or honestly," practicing "every kind of forgery and imposture" (quoted in Palmer 2004). Macpherson had also been heavy in editing; nevertheless he was accessing a genuine Gaelic literary tradition. Percy's work did become a key component in European literary culture: "Poetry has been absolutely redeemed by it," claimed William Wordsworth in his *Essay supplementary to the Preface, Lyrical Ballads* (1815, 75).

Stuart Piggott, a very English prehistorian who established his archaeological career in the 1930s under the patronage of Alexander Keiller, the Scottish "Dundee Marmalade" millionaire, and went on to become Abercrombie Professor of Archaeology at Edinburgh, provides an analysis in his collection *Ruins in a Landscape* (1976) of Walter Scott's (depictions of) antiquarianism. He finds three components. The first is an empirical orientation: this is the somewhat mundane concern of collectors for the attributes, provenance and provenience of the objects in their collections, an aspiration to be accurate and precise in the catalog, or in the documentation of a region's antiquities and its natural history. The second component is the romantic. Piggott says little of this interest, assuming the link between antiquarianism and the Romantic movement to be well understood: it is to be found, for example, in Scott's Gothic taste, his fondness for national character types and the picturesque landscapes of the national past. Piggott connects the work of Percy and Macpherson with such romanticism. The great value of Piggott's essay is in his identification of the third component: what, in 1794 Dugald Stewart, moral and political philosopher, Professor at Edinburgh, termed "Theoretic or Conjectural History."

This eighteenth century movement, this set of debates may, under this designation, sound highly esoteric, but it was a key component of the Scottish Enlightenment and has had the most profound effect upon the disciplines of anthropology and archaeology right up to the present. Theoretic or Conjectural History was a response to questions about the development of human society, institutions and language. It is actually very familiar and refers to evolutionary schemes that lie behind history and human development. The French Montesquieu had considerable influence with his distinction between stages of savagery and barbarism, the shift from dispersed savage clans to small nations, capable of being united. Adam Smith held that the "gradual progress of man from the savage state always seems to follow the same pattern, beginning with hunting and fishing, advancing to flocks and herds, and then to agriculture and commerce" (quoted by Piggott, 1976, 153). Hugh Blair, Professor of Rhetoric and Belles-Lettres at Edinburgh, was not alone in seeing four stages in the sequence of human evolutionary development: hunting and fishing, pasturage, agriculture, and commerce. Monboddo introduced a causative principle: population pressure, precipitating agriculture, the invention of language, and finally the state of civility and arts, represented by ancient civilizations known from history. The basis for these schemes could not be historical sources. Monboddo explains: "I have been at great pains to collect Facts from travelers both dead and living, and to compare these with the facts related by the ancient authors" (Blair and Monboddo, quoted by Piggott, 1976, 152). Theoretic or Conjectural History was based upon ethnographic analogy, reports coming from overseas colonies.

Blair wrote a critical dissertation supporting Macpherson's Ossian in 1765, and argued that poetry was a product of the earliest stages of human evolution, once language was achieved: "in order to explore the rise of poetry, we must have recourse to the deserts and the wilds; we must go back to the age of hunters and the shepherds; to the highest antiquity" (quoted by Piggott 1976, 156; I have been unable to trace the original). Macpherson provided such a poet from the highest of antiquity. Scott, in his Introduction to the *Minstrelsy of the Scottish Borders,* his own collection of ancient poetry, makes the same connection: "the more rude and wild the state of society, the more general and violent is the impulse received from poetry and music. The Muse records in the lays of inspiration, the history, the very religion of savages" (Scott 1802, xc). This is the significance of the voice of the past. Antiquarian collection brings us to confront the origins, the very character of human being. The project was not just to establish local, national, or cultural origins, English, Scottish, Border. In question was the original character and origin of humanity itself.

Unfortunately Piggott's history of antiquarian thought is what is still sometimes called a Whig history (after Butterfield 1931). He only respects what he considers to be the most progressive aspects of antiquarian practice, the "empirical, questioning, practical; heir to the lucidity and formality of classical thought and language." He despises what he calls the romantic sensibility of Scott, the poet and storyteller. He considers Theoretic or Conjectural History entirely speculative and so useless, attributable to "the Scottish taste for claret no less than philosophical discussion" (Piggott 1976, 152). Piggott reads history from his present, teleologically, with Scott, Smith, Monboddo and Stewart judged according to how far they had advanced towards Piggott's own judgment of himself. He views history as driven by an aspiration to progress, and anachronistically looks for leading lights, the great minds that carried ideas forward, in the face of what is *now* seen as suspect or shaky. As a result, his insights turn into a caricature that misses the deep articulation of his three components.

Mary Poovey follows Jerome Christensen in her illustration of deep intricacy in David Hume's own take on Theoretic or Conjectural History. The argument occurs in her great interdisciplinary book *A History of the Modern Fact* (1998) which explores the conceptual roots of modern systematic knowledge. On page 229 she is discussing Hume's *A Treatise of Human Nature: Being an Attempt to introduce the experimental Method of Reasoning into Moral Subjects (1739–40).* Hume offered two models of historiography, *both* examples of experimental method. The first uses as evidence the unanimous testimony of historians that can be traced back in an unbroken chain to the testimony of those who were eyewitnesses and spectators. The second model has no such unbroken chain of evidence. Typically in this model, the events in question, such as the origins of language or society, occurred before written records of eyewitness spectators were kept. For Hume, the gaps can be filled with general postulates about human nature derived from introspection, speculation, and observation. However, this filling of gaps is actually a dilemma intrinsic to the collection of any kind of evidence. It even applies, for example, to the formulation of knowledge on the basis of gathered data. The lack of a chain of evidence exemplifies the basic problem of induction for Hume, because the breaks in any chain of evidence require extrapolation, by which one assumes that unobserved phenomena will resemble what one has already seen. Hume calls this extrapolation a *belief in system*. Without it there could be no general knowledge. Imaginative proposition of a general system or structure fills in the gaps between evidence; poetry is necessary. There is, he contends, no necessary contradiction between the painstaking accumulation of facts, and speculative, poetic and fictional leaps of imagination that can, particularly through metaphor and analogy, connect what we observe (or what we deductively propose) with systems (of these various derivations) that give those observations meaning. This case for the combination and complementarity of empirical argument and a poetry of system building comes from one who is usually credited with being a most hard-headed and skeptical of empiricists. Nor was he alone in this. Philosopher and political economist Adam Smith recognized that what he called the "Poeticall method" was essential to robust argument, performing the same function as in Hume's experimental method, that of bridging gaps in chains of historical evidence, as well as answering a desire for systematic and coherent historical narrative or model (Poovey deals with Smith in her chapter 5).

Was it Georg Lukács who commented that a good historical novel assures the reader that the past might have indeed been that way, that a better novel makes a more convincing case that the past was indeed as the novel describes, but that the best historical novels are those that impress upon the reader that the past *should* have been as described?

Worldbuilding is a key activity in the archaeological imagination: filling in the gaps to create a convincing world, perhaps claiming realist validity, or perhaps content to remain fantastical. Tolkein is paradigm of a whole genre of fantasy literature, now the main component of a massive global gaming and entertainment industry. Tolkein set out to create a mythical tradition set in an Anglo-Germanic cultural imaginary, populated with monsters and heroes, referencing a deep time lost to conventional history, when men fought alongside elves. Such worldbuilding is powerfully familiar because it makes use of the kinds of cultural archetypes identified in the likes of the comparative mythology of Joseph Campbell, or more analytically in narratology (see below). Archaeology always has to creatively fill the gaps between the sources; there are no unbroken chains of evidence connecting us to antiquity and prehistory.

To return to Edinburgh. My point is not that Hume or any of these others in the Scottish Enlightenment got it right about human history or the character of human society. Rather, like those of an archaeological disposition now, they were dealing with matters such as the reconciliation of imperfect evidence from the deep past with a desire to reconstruct, the development of an experimental method that could be applied to questions of human nature and origin. Frankly, today we struggle to be as sophisticated as Hume and Smith; it can be seriously doubted that we have come much further, even after two centuries and more of archaeological discoveries! (A serious treatment of this suspicion has been offered by Bruno Latour and Shirley Strum in their article *Human social origins: Oh please, tell us another story!*, which first appeared in the *Journal of Social and Biological Structure* in 1986, but is now readily available on Bruno's Web site.)

Let me step back and make a comment about archaeology as such a practice of interweaving evidence local and distant, bridging gaps across past and present, and between different kinds of evidence. Archaeologists have frequently been compared with detectives. Though the familiar persona of the detective only arrives in the middle of the nineteenth century with the state's introduction of police forces and Edgar Allan Poe's literary figure of C. Auguste Dupin (in the short story of 1841 *The Murders in the Rue Morgue*), here we have reflection upon the process of gathering evidence and extrapolation. There is a lot more to this connection than the theme of piecing together a picture from fragments of evidence. The archaeological imagination is a faculty of the *metaphysical* detective, constantly doubting, balancing report against material witness, questioning the forms of representation that allow us to inquire of the past. I say *metaphysical* because this detective work takes us into *ontological* questions, questions of human being and identity, our human place in the very fabric of history. This is surely one of the attractions of the genre of detective fiction, of the character of the detective: their allegorical force. A favorite of mine is Morse (played by actor John Thaw), created by the author Colin Dexter and appearing in thirty-three TV episodes between 1987 and 2000 (originally on the UK ITV network). The convoluted plots of each of the 100 minute episodes take us as much into the classic components of literary emplotment and human experience, doubt and fallibility, as they do into worlds of crime.

2.4 *The Antiquary*

I return to the figure of the antiquary.

Walter Scott's novel *The Antiquary* was published in 1816 in the wake of Napoleon's defeat at Waterloo. The writing had been somewhat delayed by a visit Scott made to the battlefield; he brought back many pieces of armor and weaponry, still prominently displayed at his home, Abbotsford, on the River Tweed. A French invasion figures significantly in the plot, what there is of it.

The setting is the wartime year of 1794. A young Englishman, Lovel, arrives in northeast Scotland on mysterious business. He meets the locals, including the eponymous antiquary Jonathan Oldbuck, rescues the local squire and his daughter from a watery grave, and fights a duel when his identity is questioned. At the end, Lovel, who has turned out to be a lost heir, musters the locals at a false alarm of a French invasion, his identity is revealed, his aristocratic legitimacy established, and he marries the woman he loves, restoring her family fortune and his own.

It is not a strong plot; this is typical of Scott. The hero, if Lovel can even be called that, is absent for most of the novel, which consists of a slow and sometimes comic or whimsical account of the detection and authentication of several ancient buried treasures in the ruins of Saint Ruth's Priory. The setting at least establishes the link with the antiquary of the title, though Oldbuck is actually quite marginal.

Nothing is really at stake in the novel, nothing of importance seems to hang on the events of the narrative, even given its historical setting. It reads much more as a loose series of happenings and observations that actually marginalize historical events, turning them at the end into farce. *The Antiquary* celebrates everyday, provincial, ordinary, modest gossip and chitchat. Scott was quite explicit about this. He opens the work with an "Advertisement": "The present work completes a series of fictitious narratives, intended to illustrate the manners of Scotland at three different periods. *Waverley* embraced the age of our fathers, *Guy Mannering* that of our own youth, and *The Antiquary* refers to the last ten years of the eighteenth century."

So the triptych covers a generation of memory, but not historical memory, in the sense of recollection of momentous events. The novel's model of historical agency is quite different. "I have been more solicitous to describe manners minutely, than to arrange in any case an artificial and combined narrative, and have but to regret that I felt myself unable to unite these two requisites of a good novel."

Plot and history are deliberately secondary to what we might now, with Pierre Bourdieu, call *habitus*—what Scott calls manners. Scott emphasizes language, particularly the strong and direct language of the working classes: "the antique force and simplicity of their language, often tinctured with the Oriental eloquence of Scripture, in the mouths of those with elevated understanding, give pathos to their grief, and dignity to their resentment." The novel offers multiple voices, competing dialects and indeed competing genres. A glossary is supplied to decode the dialect and vernacular. Added to this polyvocality, we are given a miscellany of antiquarian jargon, legal and clerical terms, heraldic terms, along with scraps of Biblical quotation, Latin and French, and all sorts of poetry, quoted and quite obviously and deliberately misquoted.

The novel became well known for its humorous depiction of the friendly enthusiasm and follies of Jonathan Oldbuck, the antiquarian. Lovel, the lost heir, is drawn into the local community through Sandy (Alexander) Gordon's antiquarian work *Itinerarium Septentrionale*: Lovel, who shares an enthusiasm for Roman ruins, notices Oldbuck reading the handsome folio on the coach and strikes up a conversation. Later, in chapter 4, Oldbuck takes Lovel to an earthwork on his property—the supposed Roman camp at the Kaim of Kinprunes. This is one of the few settings or stages in the novel, others being the Priory ruins and Oldbuck's house.

> Oldbuck—"So you see nothing else remarkable?—Nothing on the surface of the ground?"
>
> Lovel—"Why, yes; I do see something like a ditch, indistinctly marked."

> "Indistinctly!—Pardon me, sir, but the indistinctness must be in your powers of vision—nothing can be more plainly traced—a proper *agger* or *vallum,* with its corresponding *ditch* or *fossa*. Indistinctly! Why Heaven help you! ...
>
> I appeal to people's eyesight—is not here the *Decuman* gate? And there, but for the ravage of the horrid plow, as a learned friend calls it, would be the *Praetorian* gate. On the left-hand you may see some slight vestiges of the *porta sinistra,* and on the right side one side of the *porta dextra* well-nigh entire ...

Edie Ochiltree, the local licensed beggar, "the news carrier, the minstrel, and sometimes the historian of the district" (page 47) arrives at the scene. He dismisses Oldbuck's interpretation and declares the earthwork to be the grassed over remains of a building thrown up by his friends for a local wedding. He personally remembers the occasion: "I mind the bigging o't."

Oldbuck and Ochiltree dispute the interpretation of an inscription dug up at the site. The stone bears the letters ADLL and a carving of what looks to be a handled cup. Oldbuck interprets the lettering to be an abbreviation of the Latin *Agricola Dicavit Libens Lubens* (Agricola [the Roman general] dedicated this freely and generously) and the cup to be a sacrificial vessel. Edie corrects him—one of the mason lads at the wedding carved the stone, depicting a ladle for the wedding punch, and ADLL, which stood for *Aiken Drum's Lang Ladle*. Here again are those contrasts between voice, memory and text that I covered in the previous section that discussed the voice of the bard.

Oldbuck has turned this earthwork, the Kaim of Kinprunes, this productive agricultural pasture, his own valuable landed property, over to being a monument to a grand history of war, conquest and imperialism: Agricola, Roman General, leading his legions upon a war of conquest of Caledonia, later celebrated in a work of the great Roman historian Tacitus. Edie, a mendicant beggar with no property to his name, a *gaberlunzie* in the vernacular, instead recalls it as the remains of a wedding party, an ephemeral and popular occasion in his youth.

Oldbuck, the antiquarian, is surrounded by old objects and writings, history become artifact and personal property. Here is Scott's description of his study (page 33): "The floor, as well as the table and chairs, was overflowed by the same *Mare Magnum* of miscellaneous trumpery, where it would have been as impossible to find any individual article wanted, asked to put it to any use when discovered."

Oldbuck's bibliophilia is similarly focused upon writing as artifact, upon history experienced as property, as inheritance, as family genealogy. This dubious scholarly history is counterposed to Edie Ochiltree's living history rooted in memory and voice, and concerned with lived everyday experience, the quotidian rather than overdramatized narrative.

Scott calls all this a set of fictitious narratives. Nevertheless, the apparatus of the novel obscures the fiction with scholarly commentary and citation of historical sources in the body of the narrative and in Scott's notes, even when these turn out to be false. In the expanded *Advertisement* that appeared in the definitive Magnum Opus edition of 1829, he felt it important to reassert that Oldbuck was a type and not a real person. Piggott, whom I discussed in the previous section, was fastidious in tracing the origin of Scott's antiquarian; but any models or antecedents in earlier novels are *literary* figures. True, a visit to Scott's home Abbotsford quickly confirms that the character of Oldbuck involved a great deal of self-mockery on Scott's part. But the only actual historical character in *The Antiquary* is Edie Ochiltree. This is again presented in the *Advertisement* to the 1829 edition. Edie was Andrew Gemmells, whom Scott knew and deeply respected. You can still visit his grave in Roxburgh cemetery. This returns us to the opening statement of the novel, that it is an illustration of the manners of Scottish communities; this historical novel aspires to being what we might now call ethnography, more precisely docu-drama. Authenticity lies in the dramatization of quotidian detail. And such a project, for Scott, immediately implicates the reception of the past, through memory, ruins, artifactual remains and texts or inscriptions. The irony is that the heart of the novel is this question of history, that

Figure 3 Witness and *habitus*. Market, Thessaloniki, 2006.

is the relation between past and present, but there is no coherent historiographical narrative to be found in *The Antiquary*.

There is no resolution to the novel that can be called authentic. Irony and doubt abound, just as we cannot distinguish from the background of everyday life any true subject of history, any coherent account in this narrative of a historical moment of the end of the eighteenth century. The only serious contender for someone who has actual historical agency is Edie the *gaberlunzie*; he sees through the pomposity, subterfuge and pretense, but has nothing save his wits. The end of the novel combines the spurious establishment of genealogy and inheritance, of ownership, wealth and proper place in (Scottish) society with the farce of the false alarm of a supposed French invasion. This is Scott's history: he anticipated by a century and a half the themes of the long-running BBC comedy series *Dad's Army* with its *sympathetic* mockery of the heroic narratives of the Second World War through parochial stories of the Warmington-on-Sea Home Guard—the senior-citizen local defense volunteers (http://www.imdb.com/title/tt0062552/ and http://www.bbc.co.uk/comedy/dadsarmy/). Sympathetic, because in these ambiguities and contradictions of historical sources, memory and personal identity (national and local) lie the possibility of what Scott celebrated as *home*.

In 1987 Chris Tilley and I published a critique of *Beamish: The Living Museum of the North*, a folk museum in the North East of England, on the grounds that it presented an ideological objective correlative for a false local or regional identity, one that occluded the real history of the industrial north. Objects and buildings were used, we argued, to create a nostalgic mythology of the region at its economic and heroic height in Victorian times, an experience authorized by the very materiality and immediacy of the artifacts, by property (Shanks and Tilley 1987a, 83–86). There is little historical narrative or plot in the museum: it comprises reconstructed buildings from around the north populated with artifacts from the nineteenth and early twentieth centuries and by museum guides, typically in period dress. Visitors experience the old town, the railway station, home farm, colliery village through immersion in their material environments: you can drink a pint of ale in the public house, interior circa 1925, ride on a steam locomotive, circa 1850. We commented that the museum makes much of connections with the past, and the way things, and ways of life, endure, and this is just what I now emphasize. I suggest that such heritage sites frequently work on the *ambience* of the past: the past's *habitus*, as defined above, Scott's manners, as embodied in things and environments. It is in the details of everyday life that the past seems to come alive and carry authenticity. This is in contrast to any historical narrative or drama of, say, the triumphs of entrepreneurs such as local engineers George and Robert Stephenson, pioneers in the railway industry (the northeast of England was the setting for the first passenger railway from Stockton to Darlington).

Narrative, or, more precisely plot, is often taken as a key aim of historiographical or archaeological study—a story of what happened. In this model of practice, the archaeologist sifts through the remains for evidence, distinguishing source material, signs of what happened, from the background of irrelevancy, the matrix of earth, rubble, silt, that contains the evidence, and from which the evidence is to be recovered. This background might be called the *noise of history*, against which is distinguished what actually happened, the drama, if you like: the relationship is the one in information science between signal and noise. But this model of archaeological practice is flawed if it is not recognized that there is no drama (signal) without the incidental ambience and manners (noise), in the way I have just outlined for Beamish museum.

Reenactment of Roman military and early medieval (dark age Saxon and Viking) life is popular in the UK. Every summer ancient castles and abbeys host many weekend gatherings of enthusiasts who dress and live as in the past. Their commitment to authentic detail can be very impressive and, while they may perform some dramatic diorama for the public (my family witnessed a Viking raid on the holy island of Lindisfarne some summers ago), their enthusiasm is driven by this commitment to *habitus*, manners, and the quotidian detail of armor and weaponry, tools and clothes, cuisine and cooking pots—material culture. The movie *The Eagle* (2010), about a Roman legion lost in the barbarian north beyond the border of the province Britannia, is an example of mainstream media that pays great attention to getting the details right. Lindsay Allason-Jones of Newcastle University was the archaeological consultant and concurs that the production team cared deeply about what we might call this physiognomy of the past. It works: the movie feels right to the expert eye, and it could well have looked like this in the past, whatever the formulaic plot. Contrast Hollywood movies in their heyday. Elizabeth Taylor, Richard Burton, Rex Harrison in *Cleopatra* (1962): a good deal less about the past, I suggest.

2.5 *Roman Boots*

Unlike Jonathan Oldbuck, Scott's antiquary, Sandy Gordon knew his Roman camps from the ground up. His *Itinerarium Septentrionale: A Journey thro' most of the Counties of Scotland and those in the North of England,* mentioned already above, was published through private subscription in 1726. It deals with the Romans in the north and goes into great detailed description of the surviving remains of camps and ruins in Scotland, and of Hadrian's Wall.

Here is a sample (from page 73):

> After this, both the *Praetenturae* pass by a Place called *Portgate,* where I saw the great *Roman Watling-Street* cross the Walls here. About 1356 Paces more Westerly, is another watchtower 66 Foot square. At this place both Walls are extraordinary conspicuous, about 26 Paces distant from one another.
>
> A little beyond this, they come within 13 Paces of each other, where I found another Watch-Tower of Dimensions like those already describ'd.
>
> The Ditch on *Severus's* Wall, is here 25 Feet in Breadth, and 20 Foot in Depth.
>
> Further West is likewise a Watch-Tower of the ordinary Dimensions of 66 Foot square. From this the two Walls run vastly great to a Village called *St. Oswald on the Hill Head,* keeping within 13 Paces of one another, defending the high Ground, to a few Houses called the *Wall Side,* then through a Place called *Brunton on the Wall.*
>
> Thence to the Bank of the River called *North-Tine,* at *Chollar-Ford,* are the Vestiges of a *Roman* Bridge to be seen; the Foundation of which consists of large square Stones, linked together with Iron cramps. But this Bridge however, is only seen when the Water is low.
>
> Beyond it a little way are the Vestiges of a great *Roman* station, called the *East Chesters;* which Place, according to the Rout of Stations, *per Lineam Valli,* I think may have been *Hunnum,* where the *Ala Saviniana* lay, and is the Fifth Station from the Beginning of the Wall at *Segedunum;* this Fort is likewise exhibited in my great Map .

The work is dominated by this kind of description, counterbalanced by many plans and drawings of inscriptions, and a fold-out map. Gordon literally paces out and records every boot-marked trace of remains in his itinerary. He might not have jumped off the Wall, just as Scott warned Ritson, but you can almost hear every crunch of his boots through the pages of his expensive folio.

A native of Aberdeen and successful operatic tenor on the Italian stage, Gordon makes clear in the *Preface* his familiarity with Italian collections, classical monuments, and the Renaissance and baroque buildings of Rome, Naples, and Venice. The *Itinerarium* sets the "northern journey" in the context of accounts in ancient texts of the Romans in the north. I have already mentioned that Gordon had an agenda that colors the whole work. It is a kind of political antiquarianism where the Roman walls, camps, inscriptions, and sundry excavated finds are marshaled alongside historical texts in an argument intended to achieve moral advantage for Scotland over England. Gordon saw parallels between, on the one hand, the ancient Caledonians and Romans and, on the other, the post-union north Britons and "Roman" Englishmen of his own day. In 1725, through his friendship with William Stukeley, he joined the Society of Knights in London, a circle of gentleman scholars interested in the study of Roman Britain, in contrast to the growing fascination with the Gothic, and as celebrated by the Society of Antiquaries (to which he was also elected, rising to take up the post of Secretary in 1735).

The engravings in the *Itinerarium* are revealing. Gordon illustrates many rectangular monuments in their various relationships with straight Roman roads. The monuments are all unexcavated and comprise simply earthen features—tumbled down overgrown ramparts (reminiscent again of the Kaim of Kinprunes). Gordon's illustrations mark out nothing except rectangles and lines; though they have, significantly, been paced-out. The engravings of sculpture show only sketched-in figures, focusing instead on the transcription of the inscribed text. And Gordon certainly knew his Roman authors.

Because of this lack of richness, and in spite of all the detail provided by the counted paces, the *Itinerarium* reads as a thin account, dominated by the boots, the linear arrangements of imperial Roman monuments, and lines of text. The list of subscribers was an impressive one, including all the significant learned aristocracy of the day. But the general opinion was that Gordon's work had been published too soon, and was eclipsed by Horsley's account of Roman Britain, published only a few years later. Even his patron, Sir John Clerk of Penicuik, second baronet and baron of the exchequer in Scotland, with whom Gordon had surveyed Hadrian's Wall in 1724, regularly excused Gordon's failings in one way or another by saying simply that he had done well for one of his background and education.

William Hutton was another walker. A successful Birmingham businessman, bookseller, paper merchant, and speculator in real estate, he was also an enthusiastic amateur historian and poet, best known for his *History of Birmingham* (1782), a spirited portrait of the great commercial and industrial town in the most vigorous phase of its growth. Annual walking holidays from then on provided the material for many historical and topographical accounts. The death of his wife Sarah in 1796 brought a temporary hiatus to his walking. He also began a new writing project. *Memorandums from memory, all trifles and of ancient date* (Birmingham City Archives, MS 467141), is a calendar of memories. For each day of the year Hutton recorded an incident that he remembered as having occurred on that date, choosing, when two or more incidents were remembered for the same day, the more remote and insignificant.

In 1801 when 78 years old he walked from Bennet's Hill, his home in Birmingham, north to Penrith in Cumbria, and then east along the length of Hadrian's Wall and back again—601 miles in thirty-five days in hot summer weather. His gait, described by his daughter Catherine, looked like a saunter, but was a steady two-and-a-half miles an hour. He was nearly 5 feet 6 inches tall, of stocky build, and inclined to corpulence, with a large head and a youthful look; he could still walk twelve miles with ease at the age of 88. The tour was the basis for his *History of the Roman Wall* of 1802. In complete contrast to Gordon,

Hutton makes it clear at the beginning that he wanted nothing to do with bookish learning. He mostly wrote about the locals with whom he lodged, their hospitality, or lack of it. Hutton's history is not about the past at all: his earnest concern is with the contemporary state of preservation of the Wall. I have mentioned how the Borders had been opened up by road building from the 1750s. Agricultural improvement brought new farms and greater prosperity. Roman sites suffered as an easy source of worked stone. Hutton recorded what was left of the Wall, noted the constant dilapidation, and, on at least one occasion, intervened to stop a farmer using the Wall's stone for a new house.

Both Gordon and Hutton, in different ways, foreground direct experience of the archaeological past. Gordon, in his Preface, is at pains to stress that his work is one of the improvement of reason and the pursuit of knowledge, and explicitly associates "Archiology, which consists of Monuments, or rather Inscriptions, still subsisting" with secure proof "of those facts which are asserted in History." Both focus on the immediacy of the past, on encountering what remains for contemporary human purpose: "Knowledge ought, therefore, to be one of the great and main Scopes of our Lives, which by Nature are but short and uncertain, and, consequently, should be spent with all possible Assiduity to qualify ourselves in Things becoming the dignified Natures of Rational Beings," as Gordon put it. Hutton was more interested in memory, the actuality of the past, the interruption of the past in the present. Both offer witness accounts, secured in the authenticity of perambulation.

Gordon and Hutton are early exemplars of a passion for walking and touring that offers direct encounter, an authentic immediacy. We see this also in the growth in the nineteenth century of walking in nature, in the boots of Scottish-American naturalist and preservationist John Muir, and then in the UK in the Ramblers Association. *Being there* is vital and energizing: *presence* is the key. *Going there* is, of course, the defining feature of the tourist economy that grew exponentially from the early nineteenth century. The dynamic interplay in the archaeological imagination, already mentioned with regard to the figure of the witness, is between presence and *mediation*, between the presence of the past and accounts and representations made of it. Antiquarians pioneered many of the features of the illustrated book: simply browse Alain Schnapp's account *Discovery of the Past* (1996) for examples. Photography and cartography were eagerly embraced by archaeologists in the nineteenth century (see Olsen, Shanks, Webmoor, Witmore 2012, chapter 6). Architectural software, virtual reality reconstruction, and Geographic Information Systems are principal components of contemporary archaeological technique. I suggest that there is a pronounced technophilia in archaeology because of the quest to capture as much of the presence of the past as is possible: technology offers rich media capture.

A broader and modernist dynamic surrounds, of course, the recording, capture, and mediation of live performance: over the last two centuries from live theater to phantasmagoria, to still and moving images, to radio and TV, video and multimedia. Our digital lives today are dominated by mixed media realities of multiple mediated sources, voices, presences. Archaeology is a paradigm of the challenge to capture and document experience, in all its nuanced and sensory detail, on the basis of *what comes after the event* (Giannachi, Kaye, Shanks 2012).

2.6 Itinerary and Natural History

In 1769 John Wallis published, by subscription, the two volume *Natural History and Antiquities of the County of Northumberland.* It is a somewhat archaic treatment of this county on the English side of the border with Scotland, much in the style of the seventeenth century English county chorographers such as Plot and Dugdale. Volume One has chapters on the air, the earth, sand and stone, waters, birds, plants, animals, reptiles, fish, and the character of the people, an almost alchemical treatment. The antiquities of the county are dealt with in the second volume via three itineraries, transecting the region.

These are not quite actual journeys that are being described; this is a convenient and very conventional trope, an organizing device that takes Wallis back through chorography to the Roman itineraries that are one of the earliest sources for his antiquarian scholarship. There are no maps, no illustrations. Considerable use is made of the list or catalogue. There is no narrative structure to this regional treatment, though stories and scenarios abound. The topic of chorography is the heterogeneity of inhabitation, the rich variety of life. Wallis's purpose was again a traditional one of celebrating a region, a County, its wealth, features, and character. He very clearly addresses his audience. Of course, he knew precisely who they were. The list of subscribers that opens the first volume is a distinctive petty aristocratic "County" set of professionals, landowners, magistrates, ecclesiastics and academics; and due acknowledgment is given to his patron, the Duke of Northumberland. There was no anonymous reading public to be anticipated; the book trade in Britain had not yet taken off.

The voice of the author, John Wallis, this local Vicar of Simonburn parish, is present and gently authoritative, though not intrusive. We read of his encounters and particular observations and remarks, but these do not detract from the firmness of the substantive and empirical details that are the core of the work. Here is an example from his chapter *Of Stones* (Volume One, page 62):

> In the grounds at *Overton,* near *Simonburn,* on the state of Sir *Ralph Milbank,* of *Hannaby,* in *Yorkshire,* Bart. is a slate of a bright

> lead-colour, their surfaces extremely smooth and shining with silvery flakes of talc, the laminae distinguished at the edges by alternate deep blue, and ochreous yellow veins; the stratum fourteen inches and a half thick, faced with an irony, rusty-coloured stone, which, on being struck with a hammer, falls off like wooden laths....
>
> Both the flags and slates are impatient of the fire and frosts. In the fire they crackle, and first with a loud noise like the report of a pistol, owing to their sulphurs. Under the severity of frosts and tempests, they separate into thin leaves or plates, and moulder away. If the slates had hardness equal to their lightness and beauty, they would be the most valuable of any in the kingdom for covering houses.

Careful description accompanies a practical orientation: this stone has certain properties that would make it very useful as a roofing slate. Acknowledgement of his audience is there in the record of ownership and in the genealogies and family histories that occur throughout the whole work.

Wallis emphasizes that he worked from documentary evidence and not hearsay. He also mentions great thunderstorms and floods that he witnessed himself, certain regional characters he met. Here he is on polysyllabic echoes (Volume One, pages 7–8):

> We have two of these, very curious and uncommon. One is under the bank on the north side of the river Coquet, opposite to a farm yard by Mr. Clutterbuck's summer house, at Warkworth. It will return seven notes from a German flute in a still evening.... The other is at the same village .... It repeats the words Arma virumque cano (Virg.) very articulately, and six notes from the same instrument. The locus polysonicus seems to be the castle, from which it comes in such soft and pleasing harmony, as if the castle was enchanted, and it was the voice of a Syren.

There is one conspicuous exception to this gentle authorial presence, other than the flattering dedication at the beginning. The chapter on earth and land opens with a strong exhortation for agricultural improvement, a castigation of indolent neglect of the land. Here Wallis is clearly very much a man of the eighteenth century with an enlightened attitude towards reasoned, rational treatment of the present as well as the past.

How do you write of a region? Capture a sense of place? This is the challenge faced by John Wallis as part of a growing association from the sixteenth century in northern Europe of regional identity with land and indeed property (see, for example, Helgerson 1992 for England). Wallis is also very conscious of the importance of direct encounter: he is distinctively a live presence in the county for which he writes. As in the genre of travel writing, Wallis, presenting his itineraries, is the interlocutor, a guide. His presence is essential to the account; Wallis doesn't present a single narrative of Northumberland, but plays the role of guide and *storyteller.* I note the crucial distinction here between narrative and storytelling. Narrative is a particular structure to many media forms, involving emplotment, character, viewpoint, agency, and other features. Storytelling is the mobilization of narrative in performance (understood broadly). The storyteller engages an audience and can critically interrupt the narrative with commentary, offering location and context, alternative standpoints. So there are many voices in Wallis's chorography, and rather than explanation and definitive narrative, he presents engagement and *manifestation.*

Rebecca Solnit is a favorite cultural geographer and writer of mine. In *Wanderlust* (2001) she presented a history of walking, very relevant to my discussion in the previous chapter. *Infinite City: A San Francisco Atlas* (2010) is a remarkable project in deep mapping (Pearson and Shanks 2001) the city: a graphical/cartographic/diagrammatic manifestation of the multiplicities that are San Francisco. I suggest she is revitalizing the old genre of chorography that we see too in the work of John Wallis (see also Pearson 2007).

2.7 *The Living and the Dead*

Pompeii, February 10, 1832. Walter Scott was visiting the excavations in the company of Sir William Gell, antiquarian, topographer, and local representative of the Society of Dilettanti of London. Gell was in pain with his gout and could hardly walk. Scott was dying. Both men had to be carried around the ruins in chairs.

Gell's diary, reported in 1850 by Lockhart, Scott's son-in-law and biographer, contains the following entry:

> I was sometimes enabled to call his attention to such objects as were the most worthy of remark. To these observations, however, he seemed generally nearly insensible, viewing the whole and not the parts, with the eye, not of an antiquary, but a poet, and exclaiming frequently—" The City of the Dead," without any other remark (Lockhart 1850, 741).

Pompeii was, of course, one of the first and most remarkable of archaeological excavations: from the 1740s all manner of fabulous and ordinary, tangible and evocative remains had been unearthed, material testament to the catastrophe of the eruption of Vesuvius in AD 79 that had buried the city. Gell was a well-known antiquarian and had published on many Classical themes, particularly topography and landscape. He was an expert on Roman art and archaeology: his scholarly and descriptive account of the finds at Pompeii, prepared with the architect John Gandy (*Pompeiana: The Topography, Edifices and Ornaments*, first issued in 1817–18), was about to come out in a new edition that covered the recent excavations.

Scott, too, was a well-known antiquarian, but clearly wasn't interested in Gell's knowledge of Pompeii. Scott talked more about Gell's dog which reminded him of his own back at Abbotsford in Scotland. He spent some weeks in the Naples area, but not exploring Roman antiquities. According to Lockhart and also Scott's own diary, he sought out old manuscripts, transcriptions of local stories and legends, and started turning them into a novel about bandits.

How is this apparent clash of antiquarian perspectives to be understood? "With the eye, not of an antiquary, but a poet" commented Gell. What might this mean? It was with a work in literary antiquarianism, a scholarly edition of border ballads and poetry, the *Minstrelsy of the Scottish Border*, that Walter Scott opened his spectacular publishing career in 1802. He went on to write a series of his own epic ballads that promoted him to the heights of the relatively new commercial book trade. These were accompanied by an immense diversity of writing, and were followed by Scott's seminal series of historical novels.

The *Lay of the Last Minstrel* is a long narrative poem about Border rivalries. Scott completed a first draft while living at Lasswade in 1802 and intended it to be part of the *Minstrelsy*, but it grew too long, and he published it separately in 1805. With its picturesque imageries, convoluted love affairs, sorcery, a ghost, and even a goblin and magic book, the poem was immensely popular: sales topped 27,000 over the next decade, an extraordinary figure in the new book trade.

Here is the preface:

> The Poem, now offered to the Public, is intended to illustrate the customs and manners which anciently prevailed on the Borders of England and Scotland. The inhabitants living in a state partly pastoral and partly warlike, and combining habits of constant depredation with the influence of a rude spirit of chivalry, were often engaged in scenes highly susceptible of poetical ornament. As the description of scenery and manners was more the object of the Author than a combined and regular narrative, the plan of the Ancient Metrical Romance was adopted, which allows greater latitude, in this respect, than would be consistent with the dignity of a regular Poem. The same model offered other faculties, as it permits an occasional alteration of measure, which, in some degree, authorizes the change of rhythm in the text. The machinery, also, adopted from popular belief, would have seemed puerile in a Poem which did not partake of the rudeness of the old Ballad, or Metrical Romance.
>
> For these reasons, the Poem was put into the mouth of an ancient Minstrel, the last of the race, who, as he is supposed to have survived the Revolution, might have caught somewhat of the refinement of modern poetry, without losing the simplicity of his original

model. The date of the Tale itself is about the middle of the sixteenth century, when most of the personages actually flourished. The time occupied by the action is Three Nights and Three Days.

To give a flavor of the verse, here is William of Deloraine (Canto 1.21):

A stark moss-trooping Scott was he,
As e'er couch'd Border lance by knee;
Through Solway sands, through Tarras moss,
Blindfold, he knew the paths to cross;
By wily turns, by desperate bounds,
Had baffled Percy's best blood-hounds;
In Eske or Liddell, fords were none,
But he would ride them, one by one;
Alike to him was time or tide,
December's snow, or July's pride;
Alike to him was tide or time,
Moonless midnight, or matin prime;
Steady of heart, and stout of hand,
As ever drove prey from Cumberland;
Five times outlawed had he been,
By England's King, and Scotland's Queen.

There follows a precisely routed journey past towers and ancient remains, with the recounting of anecdotes and associations offering insights into local history, regional life and the passage of time, the temporal relationships embedded in the very landscape. Typical here is the identification of characters with land, location and deed.

Marmion, of 1808, is a poem about one of the greatest military disasters in Scottish history: Flodden Field, fought in north Northumberland in 1513, when King James IV and most of his nobles fell in a fiasco of an invasion of England. Much of it was written at Ashestiel, Scott's old house on the River Tweed. The letters to friends which preface each of the six cantos describe the effects of the changing seasons upon its scenery, bringing together past and present:

Introduction to Canto II

To the Rev. John Marriott A.M.
Ashestiel, Ettrick Forest.

The scenes are desert now and bare,
Where flourished once a forest fair,
When these waste glens with copse were lined,
And peopled with the hart and hind.
Yon thorn—perchance whose prickly spears
Have fenced him for three hundred years,
While fell around his green compeers–
Yon lonely thorn, would he could tell
The changes of his parent dell,
Since he, so grey and stubborn now,
Waved in each breeze a sapling bough!
Would he could tell how deep the shade
A thousand mingled branches made;
How broad the shadows of the oak,
How clung the rowan to the rock,
And through the foliage showed his head…
From Yair,—which hills so closely bind,
Scarce can the Tweed his passage find,
Though much he fret, and chafe, and toil,
Till all his eddying currents boil—
Her long descended lord is gone,
And left us by the stream alone.
And much I miss those sportive boys,
Companions of my mountain joys,
Just at the age 'twixt boy and youth,
When thought is speech, and speech is truth.

Even the river Tweed is personified and alive. Here is another short extract to show how Scott typically deals with landscape. It describes a journey north to the Holy Island of Lindisfarne.

Canto II

And now the vessel skirts the strand
Of mountainous Northumberland;
Towns, towers, and halls successive rise,
And catch the nuns' delighted eyes.
Monkwearmouth soon behind them lay,
And Tynemouth's priory and bay;
They marked, amid her trees, the hall
Of lofty Seaton-Delaval;
They saw the Blythe and Wansbeck floods
Rush to the sea through sounding woods;
They passed the tower of Widderington,
Mother of many a valiant son;
At Coquet Isle their beads they tell
To the good saint who owned the cell;
Then did the Alne attention claim,
And Warkworth, proud of Percy's name;
And next, they crossed themselves, to hear
The whitening breakers sound so near,
Where, boiling through the rocks, they roar
On Dunstanborough's caverned shore;
Thy tower, proud Bamborough, marked they there,
King Ida's castle, huge and square,
From its tall rock look grimly down,
And on the swelling ocean frown;
Then from the coast they bore away,
And reached the Holy Island's bay.

There is no strong narrative in these poems, as in the later novels I have already discussed: structurally the poems do not cohere. With their topic of landscape and manners, terrain, tradition, scenario and narrative fragment, names and lists, genealogies and toponymies take precedence. These features are central to that antiquarian genre of chorography I just discussed in the previous section in connection

Figure 4 Lindisfarne (Holy Island), Northumberland, 2005.

with John Wallis's *Natural History and Antiquities of Northumberland*. There are numerous digressions and anecdotes and what often seem to be pointless incidents. This is backed by a not entirely spurious scholarly apparatus of footnotes that amplify the ebullience of detail with reference to historical and antiquarian sources. Scott, as author, is there in the notes, in the prefatory epistles in *Marmion*. His presence is otherwise usually diverted into the voice of a narrator; many of his works appeared anonymously and feature multiple voices and what we would now term avatars. As indicated in the Preface to the *Lay of the Last Minstrel*, just quoted, Scott wishes to disperse into the collective voice of a rude and oral medium, the ballad. Because he suggests it is appropriate to the subject matter.

As with Wallis, this is not a landscape that can be easily mapped in a two-dimensional cartography. Wallis and Scott are not representing something that can be captured in a mimetic aesthetic, let alone a visual medium. In spite of all the specific and "authentic" details, neither Wallis nor Scott is illustrating anything in particular. Wallis spent twenty years traveling, interviewing, observing, collecting, noting, reasoning and arranging the wealth and character of a county for its well-to-do. Scott explicitly produces a performative, poetic remix that eschews mimesis. Wallis's and Scott's project is one of transcription, writing over the innumerable and ineffable particularities of place and event told and retold in conversations, recollections, poems performed.

Scott and Wallis are interested in representing the folding or topology of history and time through land and place that make community. There is no surface or spatial geometry in their engagement with place that can be navigated or mapped consistently. Wallis's itineraries are organizing devices, gathering assemblages of places, people, events. An itinerary is a journey performed. It is William of Deloraine riding out to Melrose; it is the character of Northumberland revealed in a mingling, a percolation of the particulars of natural history, genealogy, ruins, antiquities, folklore, stone, water and earth. In contrast, Alexander Gordon could present a map. He had an argument to make, an axe to grind about Scottish pride, and it was about civility and barbarism, marked on the land itself in the military works of Roman legions walked again by his boots.

Scott's historical novels also pursue this topology of past, present, memory and retelling. *The Tale of Old Mortality* (1816) is set in 1679 against the backdrop of the military campaign waged by John Graham of Claverhouse's government forces against an army of Covenanters, religious rebels objecting to Episcopalian church government. The notes indicate that Scott was very familiar with seventeenth century historical sources, though the novel presents the account as being the memories of "Old Mortality." This was another local character that Scott had met (like Edie Ochiltree in *The Antiquary*), an impoverished stonemason called Robert Patterson, who had spent forty years cutting and restoring gravestones for the Covenanting martyrs, and who died in 1801. His memories are reported by a narrator. There is more to this complex framing. The novel is part of a trilogy: *Tales of My Landlord.*

Scott was not writing under his own name, but adopted various guises. In the Advertisement to *The Antiquary*, his previous novel, he had announced that its author, whose real name was unknown to the public, was retiring. Within months, however, Scott had reappeared in the guise of Jedediah Cleishbotham, schoolmaster and parish-clerk of the fictional town of Gandercleuch. Cleishbotham purported to be editing or working up stories originally sketched by a younger colleague, the late Peter Pattieson. These, in turn, were supposed to be based on tales told to Pattieson by the landlord of the local Wallace Inn, hence *Tales of My Landlord*. Scott offers the reader a *mise-en-abyme*, stories within stories within stories and set in an apparatus of intertextual commentary and criticism.

I mention the distinction I made previously between narrative and storytelling. Scott disrupts narrative form through voice and retelling, refusing a single or coherent narrative or drama to history. Central to the disruption is memory, the way the past lingers and is transmitted. In his archaeological sensibility this is duration and actuality.

Old Mortality is about the experiences of Henry Morton, a moderate Presbyterian, in the dramatic religious turmoil of 1679. It is made very clear that neither side was in the right: there are evil characters on both sides, accounts differ, and Morton is caught up in events over which he has little control. There are no simple narratives in this kind of history; *everything* was and is convoluted.

In the wake of eighteenth century Enlightenment and Revolution, radical ruptures in relationships to the past, perhaps it's not unexpected to find deep reflection upon the shape of history, and its relationship to individual experience, to individual agency, to representation and retelling. Most of Scott's historical novels (1814 onwards) certainly revolve around themes of the logic of history, personal motivation, the entanglement of affairs in individual experience, and how it may all be told. This is what makes them so human. Scott's tactic is to witness in many varied ways the convolution or topological folding of history and geography. This is the significance of the intermingling of the dead and the living, of voice and memory, of the associations between location, people and event, such that

Scott's Border landscapes are always collections of *place/events.* The question of the subject of history, of what drives history in a narrative sense (what actually happened and why) is answered by indeterminacy, by diversion and digression, detour and avoidance. Because there is always more: the real subject of history is always customs and manners, *habitus,* the background noise of what, with hindsight, get called historical events.

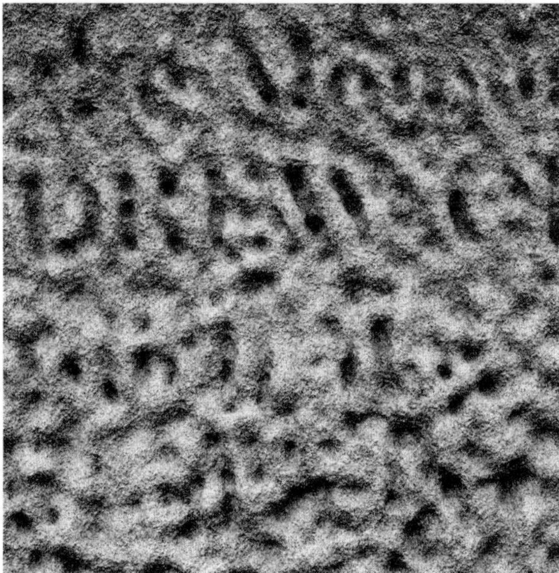

Figure 5 Epigraphy. St Aidan's, Bamburgh, 2005.

Scott reveled in all this. The "wizard of the north," as he was popularly called, dealt in the uncanny, the ways that the past comes back to haunt the living, the ways that places contain their pasts, reminding us of half-forgotten happenings. In Pompeii he sounded a final melancholy note: there was nothing to discuss about the dead there (and Scott himself was dead by the end of the year). One massive event, the destruction of the city in AD 79, had cut through history, severing the connections. Where were the memories, the ghosts? There was no continuity for Scott, no chains of memory, retellings of retellings. The relics were dry and dead. Period. The trauma of the event had left such a trench and void that they could not be bridged.

This is also a dark sepulchral note, an association of death and graves, death and exhumation in the work of the antiquarian or archaeologist. The Gothic connection is obvious and was commonplace by the early nineteenth century. From the late 1820s Edgar Allan Poe was able to create a whole world of antiquarian horrors: the fall of great families and even civilizations (poem: *The City in the Sea*), death and decomposition, being buried alive, pseudosciences offering easy answers, and the dark forensic challenge of figuring out just what is going on around us (short stories: *The Murders in the Rue Morgue* and *The Purloined Letter*).

Some years earlier, Shelley, in his poem *Ozymandias* (1818), presented a returning traveler, "from an antique land," who tells of the shattered remains of a colossal statue, set up originally to boast of the power of its subject, Ozymandias, King of Kings (the pharaoh Ramesses II of New Kingdom Egypt). "Nothing beside remains." Again, loss, even traumatic loss, is connected with agency—the power to affect history. "Look on my works, ye Mighty, and despair!" In *Prometheus Unbound* (1820) Shelley offers a utopian vision of a new world of liberation, of the imaginative spirit operating communally and outside of time. He describes the ruin of previous civilization as crushed, packed, crammed layers, geologically stratified deposits. This is one of the first explicitly archaeological images in modern poetry. History is here a material weight, "jammed in the hard black deep" (line 302), "sepulchred emblems" (line 294), that are nevertheless the foundation for freedom rooted in the future—in hope, "till hope creates from its own wreck the thing it contemplates" (lines 573–4).

These sepulchral articulations of crushing death, ruin and memory, but also of hope for freedom in the future, an aspiration to matter, to make a difference, point to a paradox in the archaeological imagination. In order to preserve the past, it must be creatively reused, even destroyed. And herein lies an archaeological anxiety, that in order to know the past, we dig, we intervene and destroy. This paradox is explicitly sepulchral, as realized by Shelley. Exhumed remains of the past can be brought back to life. Or not: they may remain dead, as in Scott's Pompeii. The paradox contains a political challenge or exhortation, that the past be taken up and redeemed. For Scott and Shelley, redemptive power lay in poetry, the work of the constitutive imagination.

Without the poetry, there is nothing to depict. There are only ever crammed layers of remains and sepulchred emblems. The pivot of the paradox is the notion of *the abject*. The abject is what generates anxiety, even nausea, because it doesn't fit; the abject is both/and, interstitial. The abject is situated outside the symbolic order, outside categories that make sense of the world, and being forced to face it can be an inherently traumatic experience. For example, in a corpse we recognize the form that the living take, but also that it is now mere raw flesh, about to rot and putrefy. A corpse is something that should be alive but isn't, and to confront its materiality is to confront the reality that we too will die and rot. The abject here is a state of being/non-being, entropy/negative entropy, life/death. It is our repulsion from the abject that confirms categories, here the boundary between the living and the dead, and so constitutes sense, helps form us as living beings.

This is the topic again of ontological security in contemporary society. One particular implication of archaeology in risk society is that, as part of the pervasive construction of risk objects, it is a system of practice and knowledge, a discourse of dealings with otherness, alterity, the abject. I refer to the potential anxiety elicited in dealing with other cultures and times that present questions of difference, challenges to establish understanding, to translate and establish common ground. The centrality of entropic processes in archaeology, decay and loss, the erosion of order and form, makes this dealing with otherness particularly sharp and challenging. It's not just that an antiquarian or archaeologist may raise questions of historical and cultural continuity, asking "is this the way we were?"; but the rot and ruin, the debris of humanity in the decaying garbage heap that is history, may mean that we may never know, that no sense may ever be established.

Figure 6 *Memento Mori*. Daguerreotype, 1850s, USA. Photographs of the deceased were quite common in the early days of photography. Photographer unknown.

The ruin and loss may even tend to nausea, an aspect of the abject: the loss of the past may be sickening; mortal flesh rots; and, without a past, we may never know who we were, or worse, who we *are*. This struggle in the face of perpetual perishing is a distinctively archaeological dimension to contemporary threats to ontological security—"City of the dead. City of the dead."

Contemporary popular culture, and indeed contemporary art (Spooner 2007, Williams 2007), continues to adore variations on the themes of the archaeological gothic. Stephenie Meyer's massively successful *Twilight* saga (from 2005) unites Byronic romance with the vampire genre of uncanny horror, as teenage Bella is haunted by the unearthly love of undead Edward Cullen, from a family of vampires reaching back into history, constantly facing the question of the identity of her own humanity. Horror combines with forensic archaeology in the Fox TV series *Bones,* which entered its seventh series in 2011. Another classic detection duo of crime fiction, one of whom is portrayed as a crime mystery author, deals with gruesome murders, treating the abjection of corporeality and decayed victims' remains with a rather dark humor and irony.

Less gothic is an obsession in the United States with family genealogy and ancestry: there is a major cultural industry (typified in ancestry.com) offering tools to build family trees, to track back family connections. In a nation of immigrants, traditional roots can easily be severed. Family pasts, rooted in genealogy rather than grand historical narrative, are a means to reestablish chains of connection that secure contemporary identity.

2.8 *Media, Representation, and* Mise-en-scène

Let's return to the Mediterranean and Scott's problem with William Gell.

Gell had made quite a reputation with his topographical studies, locating Greco-Roman antiquities and ancient sites within their landscapes. *Topography of Troy* (1804) is an early and key work in the search for the ancient site of Troy. It takes the form of annotated illustrations, presented as engraved plates of the landscapes on the plain of Troy in northwestern Anatolia. Troy of the legendary Trojan War had been lost for millennia and maybe had never existed, though it was recalled, of course, in the epics of Homer, and there was a Roman town of *Ilium* (one of its ancient names). The purpose of Gell's work was to locate through scholarship the scene of that most famous siege of ancient epic and legend.

The dedication is to Georgiana, the Duchess of Devonshire (the subject of the movie of 2008):

> Madam,
>
> It is with great satisfaction that I am enabled to send you some description of a country, on the subject of which you were pleased to express an interest highly gratifying to my mind.
>
> To have succeeded in pointing out a close connexion between the Poem and the Scene of the Iliad, and thereby contributed towards the amusement of those leisure hours, which you are sometimes enabled to borrow from the more serious duties of life, and the charms of polished society, is the sincere wish of,
>
> Madam,
>
> Your Grace's Most obliged and devoted Servant,
>
> William Gell

The explicit purpose was to publish a work that solved a puzzle of Classical Mediterranean antiquity for the polished society of London.

Plate 19 of the *Topography* is a fold-out panoramic, 180 degree view from the "Tomb of Archilochus," an archaeological monument. The annotation reads as follows:

The necessity of a general view is such, that without it no very correct idea could be full of the appearance of the plain. I have here taken the liberty, which I have used on many other occasions, of extending the drawing on each side, till all the interesting objects of the country are included. The plate is of a sufficient magnitude to permit the observer to elevate the extremities of the paper on the right and left, so that, by placing the eye in the center, and turning the head towards such parts as he wishes to examine, he will have the objects in the exact direction in which they appear to a person on the spot. It will be necessary for those, who find a difficulty in comprehending with the eye more than 60° at the same time, to consider this view, as composed of three separate pictures; as by the map it may be seen, that it includes somewhat more than 180°. The battle of Lodi, and some other pictures, have been exhibited in London under the same circumstances. The whole being taken with the help of a protractor, the distances are almost mathematically exact. It should be observed, that the foreground represents merely the conic summit of the tumulus, the base of which, in its proper proportion, would be at least 6 feet in diameter, and a figure standing on it would be eight or 9 inches in height. None, however, is introduced, as it would exclude some of the mountains, or part of the plain .

Figure 7 William Gell's Bounarbashi: the acropolis of Troy. From his book *The Topography of Troy* (1804).

Plate 32 (figure 7) is an illustration of the Hill of Bounarbashi, a candidate for the ancient acropolis of Troy. Gell comments:

> This drawing has nothing to recommend it except the assistance it affords to the general plan for the illustration of every part of the hill of Bounarbashi, no portion of which can be totally uninteresting to the curious. The view was taken from a window in the back part of the Aga's house looking nearly south. The two tumuli in the Acropolis are discoverable at the summit of the highest hill. Beyond the most distant house on the left, the ground falls very quickly toward the river. The city appears to have entirely covered the rising ground, and if so, must have produced a noble effect.
>
> The longhouses in the foreground are exact portraits of those which now exist at Bounarbashi, and will give an idea of such as are generally found throughout the country. I have been informed that the streets, if indeed they are worthy of that name, are paved with a species of lava, but I am not able to speak from my own knowledge on the subject.

This is quite a statement! The drawing is reproduced in a very expensive folio, and, in the edition I consulted, hand-tinted rather beautifully. But it is only of scholarly value, Gell asserts: it is otherwise boring. More precisely, and taking into account his audience, his concern is to cover the ground, as it were, to cover all angles (literally in the panoramas) such that the text and visuals take the reader on location, or, more precisely, bring the Mediterranean to the reader in England. These are not at all meant to be picturesque views or *vedute*, pictures of the great sites brought back from a Grand Tour of Italy and the Mediterranean. Even if what is illustrated is relatively uninteresting, the purpose is to offer visual evidence or documentation of what we should be interested in, if we are to count as curious scholars. Gell is somewhat sneering about the place itself: the streets are not really streets. The glorious past is what he is interested in, the noble effect of the ancient city on its acropolis, now *only to be imagined*. He mentions lava stone, but doesn't consider it necessary to check whether it is or isn't. The break between the ancient and the modern, between past and present is almost complete.

Gell clearly aimed to achieve optical consistency and accuracy. The angles in the panorama are measured by protractor and mathematically correct; you can read distances off from them. In his *Pompeiana,* mentioned in the previous section, Gell notes (Volume One, page xvi) that the illustrations were all produced with a camera lucida. This was a new optical device, patented by Wollaston in 1807, that enabled the user to split a view of a subject, such as an artifact or a building, through a prism, so that a drawing could be traced while still looking at the subject, superimposed onto paper beneath the prism of the camera lucida. The camera lucida used the hand of the draughtsman as the means to fix a projected image, the task that would be given over to stabilized light sensitive chemicals in the 1840s, with the processes developed by Daguerre and Fox Talbot.

Another of Gell's topographical works applied a different kind of empirical consistency to the landscape. His *Itinerary of Greece, with a commentary on Pausanias and Strabo, and an account of the Monuments of Antiquity at present existing in that country, compiled in the years 1801, 2, 5, 6 etc* (1810, and especially the second edition of 1827) was a book about roads. In it he records the times taken to walk between notable features of the landscape of southern Greece. Much like the navigational time logs of the period, these travel times are collated by Gell into lists. The steady movement of the cogs and gears of his pocket watch, clockwork, translates into a measure applied to his consistent pace as he walks the roads of Greece. The repetitive act of temporally referencing one's location regulated his walking, his grounded practice. The measurement of time, if procedural, if ruthlessly consistent, becomes here the measurement of physical distance. And a system of measurement of any kind is a key element in standardization and abstraction. Gell's system went a long way towards the production of a reliable map of the Peloponnesian interior of southern Greece.

This is quite unlike the itineraries of Wallis's chorography of Northumberland, or of Scott's poetry (discussed above). An itinerary for

Wallis and Scott is a journey articulated and *performed,* not an abstract vector of paces or the measured passing of time as one walks or rides.

Gell and Scott, Wallis too, shared a deep concern with the relationship between ancient sources and the present. They were concerned, but in different ways, with the historical roots of modern Europe, whether that is an English county in an era of agricultural improvement and reasoned inquiry, an emergent nation state such as Scotland, or classical roots in Greco-Roman antiquity (and Wallis has a great deal to say about Roman influences on regional character, as well as Roman remains). All three dealt in authenticity. Sometimes this authenticity lay in accurate and descriptive detail, a celebration of historical minutiae. All were keenly aware of the role of philological source criticism, sharing a scholarly and critical concern with textual authenticity.

Gell was a *topographer* in his interest in the intersection of the lay of the land and history. At the heart of his engagement with land is a consistent pace, measured by the gearing of a pocket watch, and optical consistency, measured by degrees of a protractor and the vanishing point of perspective. Both come together in the panorama and the map. The maps and panoramas in Gell's *Geography and Antiquities of Ithaca* (1807) are extraordinary accomplishments of the engraver's art. Gell also anticipated the optical properties of the photograph, even before the invention of chemical fixing of a projected image.

The county maps of Elizabethan England and after were central to the contrasting project of *chorography* (see the insightful study by Richard Helgerson in his *Forms of Nationhood,* 1992). But Saxton's famous cartography, for example, was precisely connected to the gazetteers of chorography in its toponymy, its profusion of place names. Saxton's maps may be good for finding your way because you can see which villages are next to which; what you can't do is rely on them for accurate navigation based upon geometry and scaled distance: they are too densely packed and the scale is wrong, more suited to taking in the whole rather than physical engagement. Cartography had changed in the seventeenth century, not least with the military mapping of the Borders and Highlands, already mentioned.

Gell, the topographer, has the military and administrator's eye of calculation. Gell stands over his camera lucida with the objective and detached eye of the connoisseur and traces lineaments of architecture or the outlines of an antique work of art. Wallis and Scott are not topographers in this sense. Their focus is *topology,* a different kind of involved representation or manifestation of the intermingling of place, person and event.

A critical (and archaeological) topos or rhetorical structure in the work of all these antiquarians is *place/event* or "this happened here." Again there are decisive differences between chorographers and topographers. For chorographers Wallis, Percy, and Scott, the intersection of place and event comes primarily through memory and witnessing. It is what people have done, events witnessed, stories retold and descriptions made that lie at the heart of memory practices, at the heart of human inhabitation and community. It is precisely the connection between past and present that they foreground in their work; and voice, echoing from past lives, or the presence of the author/editor. Contrast Gell: it may be that Bournarbashi, a village in Turkey, was where Achilles fell, and that we read of this in Homer, but Homer does not belong in that place now; his works have become a currency of *transcendent* cultural value. The connection between past and present for Gell, the topographer, is *diagrammatic.* Here at coordinate point x,y, triangulated upon topographical features a,b,c, died Achilles. And this knowledge can literally be transported through a certain kind of inscription and publication to the learned societies of London, and to the Duchess of Devonshire's Salon, for entertainment, edification, and scientific use. Reciting the ride of William of Deloraine won't help you navigate through the Scottish borders like a map would, but it does offer a powerful performative, rather than diagrammatic, engagement with the lay of the land.

Gell offers us optical consistency in the documentation of evidence, such that it can be taken elsewhere for standardized assessment. Let me follow up on the photographic character of certain kinds of documentation of evidence. Consider illustration. Scott's works were frequently illustrated. The *Border Antiquities,* for example, is a theatre of the picturesque, consisting mainly of engraved plates of notable sites accompanied by descriptions. I say picturesque because of the characteristic aesthetic. Each site is carefully framed (and so manipulated), as in a theater set, with foreground, middleground and backdrop. Features such as trees to left and right contain the view, as in proscenium arch and stage setting, while devices such as linear and atmospheric perspective, a road or river winding its way into the view, a distant town or range of hills in the backlit haze or mist, draw the viewer into the scene. The lighting, props, staging, blocking of these ruins in a landscape are deliberately theatrical. Illustrations in Scott's poetry and novels regularly act in this way as a separate, almost independent order of representation; they are incidental to the narrative, because they can only ever depict incidents, characters, snapshots, rather than any essence of the performative topology, the engagement with place/event, genealogy and community. There are no illustrations in Wallis's chorography of Northumberland; he didn't even try to graphically illustrate his account. The difference between Wallis and Scott is that Scott had a different and demanding audience: a new popular audience served by the new book trade that could deliver cheaper engraved imagery, an audience that was getting used to travel and wanted pictures, delivered in a comforting and familiar aesthetic, of sights worth visiting, especially when they were connected with a story or drama. As I indicated in the previous section, Wallis was writing for a narrow and very well-to-do readership committed to his writing and treatment of a world that was their property, a readership that had, through their subscription, already approved the work before publication. The village scene in Gell that I described above is part of a work completely centered upon visual representation, but it does not use a theatrical aesthetic at all; Gell's pictures demand the scrutiny of the curious, eager to figure out why Gell had actually included it in his work. The implication is that something had changed regarding ownership and property in the half century between Wallis and Gell.

Figure 8 The northern sublime: the Roman remains at Chew Green (*Ad Fines*), Upper Coquetdale, Northumberland, 2008.

Gell offers optically consistent documentation, as was later provided by photography. The tensions between these different kinds of representation are clear from the earliest of experiments in chemical photography. William Henry Fox Talbot was a pioneer, using a positive/negative process for producing paper-based photographs from the mid 1830s. *The Pencil of Nature* (1844) was the first book to be illustrated with photographs; it was intended to show the many possibilities of the new medium. It opens with an anecdote about Talbot's inability, shared with many others, to work with a camera lucida, in his case on a trip to Italy in 1833: whereas the camera lucida required the pencil of an artist to record an image, photography delegated that work to nature and chemistry. Talbot anticipated most of the future uses of photography: for documenting (objectively and authentically), for reproduction and copying (exactly and mechanically), and to produce pictorial illustration (as in landscapes and portraits). Browsing these themes through *The Pencil of Nature* is a very direct way of encountering a particular manifestation of the archaeological imagination. Archaeological themes are plentiful in early photography: the two fields clearly complemented each other.

Let me return again to place/event, the engagement with a site focused upon the question: this happened here; or did it, could it have? The pursuit of such a question comes to involve a forensic attitude at the heart of the archaeological imagination. I have already mentioned the notion of the archaeologist as metaphysical detective. The associated forensic attitude is an attitude toward location. It can be summarized as follows: *at scene of crime anything could be relevant*. And anywhere could be a scene of crime. Faced with a scene of crime, the task for the detective is to identify, gather, and analyze evidence on the basis of which may be established a forensic case. But it is by no means obvious, often, what is evidence. *Anything*, potentially, could be evidence. As Gell described his illustration: "this drawing has *nothing* to recommend it except the assistance it affords to the general plan for the illustration of *every part* of the hill ... no portion of which can be totally uninteresting to the curious" (Gell 1804, plate 32). Anything could matter. It could be that the key to a case is an overlooked fragment or trace, a hair that could be analyzed for DNA, scratches by the door made by a unique pattern of nails upon the criminal's boots. Nothing is totally uninteresting to the detective. Then there is always doubt whether there is enough evidence to warrant the reconstructed sequence of events and attribution of motivation. Evidence won't speak for itself; it needs mobilizing in a case, and this requires the detective to document the evidence.

Photography is the medium most perfectly suited to this forensic project. Let me introduce Walter Benjamin's comments on photography and the antiquarian imagination (in his *Little History of Photography* [1931], and see Carlo Salzani's very astute study, *The City as Crime*

Scene: Walter Benjamin and the Traces of the Detective, 2007). Eugène Atget photographed the streets and buildings of Paris in the late nineteenth and early twentieth century. In his essentially documentary project he collected series of views based on themes such as the ornamental features of seventeenth- and eighteenth-century buildings, signage of bars and cabarets, apartment interiors, street views. They take a documentary stance; Atget emphasizes content over his own presence to the act of photography. His photographs were intended for the use of painters, illustrators, decorators, set designers, and members of the building trades. Most of Atget's scenes are curiously empty of people, communicating an ironic stillness at the heart of urban life. You find yourself asking—why was this photo taken?

The Marxian critic and scholar of the Kabbala, Walter Benjamin, discovered Atget's photographs in the 1930s, along with the French surrealists. With others he thought that Atget photographed the streets of Paris as if they were scenes of crime. A scene of a crime, too, is deserted, as in Atget; a scene of crime is photographed for the purpose of establishing evidence. With the likes of Atget, photographs become a paradigm of evidence for occurrences. They are a paradigm, a method, or a standard, because, of course, nothing may have happened in the photographed scene to actually prompt the photograph. The potential of these spaces is enough to justify their photographic capture and documentation. They are a species of space where we ask—what happened here? As much as a focus on a past happening, this attitude towards place is about potentiality. We ask—what could have happened here? We imagine and look forward—what could happen here? Far from being empty spaces, these are place/events, with a history and a future.

Benjamin described this potentiality as a hidden *political* significance. This species of space demands a specific kind of approach; free-floating contemplation, an appreciation of the aesthetics, the balance of composition, as in a classic picturesque landscape, is not appropriate to them; "there is nothing to recommend them," again Gell's words. They stir the viewer; we feel challenged by them, but in a negative sense. Effort is needed to bridge the voids opened in this kind of space. The photographs beg for captions; Atget usually supplies them, and often they document the later demolition of a building.

Consider what happens when you don't add captions to such photographs. *Evidence* (1977) presents a project pursued by Mike Mandel and Larry Sultan. They gathered a collection of photographs from archives that document scientific and industrial research and development. They refused the obligation to supply subject matter, to complement the images with identifying captions. The photographs in their book are completely mysterious and quite surreal, often threatening and disturbing, as you ask—just what exactly was going on in these experiments? They are like stills from the *X Files* (discussed above).

Figure 9 At a scene of crime ... James Street, Cardiff, site of the murder of Lynette White in 1988.

The potentiality of any place to become a scene of crime; the indeterminacy of this species of space, that anything there could equally be classed as evidence of some sort; this reduction of the distinctiveness of site to a common ground of potential for happening and of investigation; the simultaneous and paradoxical individuation of site as a unique multiplicity of place/events, real and possible, past and future: these are characteristics of *urban* space. Such spaces are quite different from the Border communities of Scott and Wallis.

So there are important differences among chorographers, topographers, and photographers. The common ground is document and representation, the question of how to represent a community, a landscape, a place/event in the work of the archaeological imagination. I hope my examples show that different approaches to the collection of sources, critique and commentary, documentation, publication and display lead to different kinds of architectures, spaces and arrangements, geometries and connections between people, events and things. A term that captures much of this is *mise-en-scène*. I offer a definition somewhat broader than usual, and emphasizing architecture and arrangement: *mise-en-scène* is the choice of location and viewpoint, the arrangement of items and actors in front of a camera or before a recording author, setting a scene to be documented, photographed or filmed, such that the resulting account, still or movie has a certain designed outcome, makes a point, communicates a message, fits into a story, conveys the intention of the photographer or filmmaker. *Mise-en-scène* is about the disposition, arrangement and relationships between people, artifacts, places and happenings, just as I have been exploring in the world of the antiquarian. Architecture and arrangement run to the heart of *the archive*: the archive is primarily an architectural matter.

Gell looking through his camera lucida is one architectural arrangement between observer and object (think of the prism as a window). Wallis visiting and talking with his parishioners is another kind. Scott was carried around Pompeii in a chair; while in Naples he searched for old manuscripts in bookseller's stalls; at home he worked in his study and debated with guests over dinner. This is not meant to be mysterious; the architecture of record and representation can be quite mundane. Sorting evidence often needs tables and space; sorted collections need boxes and cupboards to keep them ordered. Consulting archives requires good sources of light and facilities to take notes. Museums, with their galleries, displays, arrangements, become stages for the presentation of the past. This also involves administrative apparatuses of accounting, storage, surveillance, and disbursement.

These antiquarians were seeking authenticity in their accounts and documentation: this raises questions about the author's relationship to audience and community, as well as object. Benjamin reckoned there to be hidden *political* significance in the forensic photography of urban space. A key difference between chorographers and topographers is *representation*, the *political challenge* to represent the past. By representation I do not mean simply the matter I have been discussing of illustration, description or report, but *political* representation, witnessing, speaking for others, to others. The matter of representation refers us to constituency, and to the forum or assembly of representatives. Our authors report to both. Though they may not acknowledge this, such relationships are at the core of their authorial agency. Without subscribers Gell could never have produced his handsome volumes. Without a book-buying public Scott would not have been able to live as an author.

Scott represents the Borders as an inhabitant, magistrate, popular writer, collector, landowner, member of the local yeomanry, literary antiquarian, witness. He is folded into the land as much as his characters. His presence is central to this representation, though he often works through an avatar or alias, through multiple voices. And no easy narrative encompasses his representing voice, because there is none in the heterogeneity of human inhabitation. But there are stories to be retold to new audiences in old constituencies. Pertinent here again is the distinction I have drawn between narrative and such storytelling (discussed earlier).

Though he is one of the first great economic successes of the new book trade, selling thousands of copies to an eager readership, Scott locates himself as an heir, a guardian of an old oral and literary tradition—the ballad—and thus raises questions of memory and archive.

Because of this explicit acknowledgement of the politics of representation, I have suggested that a fulcrum in his writing is indeed historical agency—people's implication in historical change. We can see this in Wallis and Percy, too, but differently; their constituency was not the new reading public. Wallis references the great characters of Northumberland marked on the land itself, and the opportunities presented to build with the riches of the land and its history. Percy is concerned with folk traditions, the mark of the people on national culture.

Gell, representative of the Society of Dilettanti, was still writing with a view to aristocratic patronage, for an international cultured elite facing the rise of an urban, industrialized and commercialized Europe. I suggest that Scott reacted to Gell's tour of Pompeii as he did and thought more of his dog back in his beloved home on the River Tweed because of the way that Gell's antiquarian study and archaeological reconstruction failed to realize that it should focus on connections between past and present, work performed upon remains, representation in a political sense of bearing witness to the life and times of located communities. The shifts towards the institutionalization and standardization of objects of discourse, the map, plan, description, regional account, and their reorientation upon a particular constituency were the core of the emerging field of professional archaeology, and, more importantly, the administrative apparatuses of the modern state in the nineteenth century. Scott rejected this shift, seeing that it destroys a living connection with the past. Archaeology, as historiography, settled through the nineteenth century into the task of establishing the timetables of unrecorded history and prehistory, with linear series of events (there was this, then this, then this). Such a project offers not chains of connection with the past, but radical lacunae, gaps in history that, in the absence of complete evidence, could never be bridged with science. Gell, ironically perhaps, embraced it. (Susan Stewart has provided some great case studies exploring this changing figure of the author, including the ballad writers, in *Crimes of Writing*, 1991.)

Representation implies speaking for another, translation and mediation. Implicated also is the transition from voice (oral poetry, verbal account, memory) to text (a new version of the old song, the annotated transcription/edition, the historical novel, historical narrative), from artifact and site to description, account and narrative. Representation in this broad sense includes questions of how the witnessing pace of the antiquarian, how sites and their names, how place/events become itinerary, chorography, cartography, or travelogue. Representation as transmission or translation is aimed precisely at establishing chains of connection and fields of association through multitemporal foldings of pasts in presents.

Conventional notions of media (as material modes of communication—print, painting, engraving, or as organizational/institutional forms—the media industries) are of limited help in understanding what Scott and his contemporaries were up to in so mediating authorial voice and authentic traces of the past, in turning the land into an illustrated book. We can consider the rise of cheaper engraved illustration, the popularity of the historical novel in the growth of the publishing industry, developments in cartographic techniques and instruments. But in order to understand how all this and more came to be archaeology—the field, social and laboratory science—we need to rethink the concept of medium.

Scott, Ritson, Gordon, Gell and their like were *making manifest* the past (or, crucially, were aiming to allow the past to manifest itself), in its traces, through practices and performances (writing, corresponding, visiting, touring, mapping, pacing, debating), artifacts (letter, notebook, manuscript, printed book, pamphlet, map, plan, as well as ancient objects themselves), instruments (pen, paint brushes, rule, camera lucida, surveying instruments, boots, wheeled transport, spades, shovels, buckets), systems and standards (taxonomy, itinerary, grid), authorized algorithms (the new philology, legal witnessing), and dreams and design (of an old Scotland, of a nation's identity, of personal achievement). Making manifest came through manifold articulations and displacements (bringing together artifacts and maps in the study or salon). Such manifestation was a complement to epistemological and ontological interest—getting to know the past *as it was, and is.*

Visual media, in the conventional sense (print, engravings, maps), are involved, but also much more. What we are seeing, I suggest, is a reworking of ways of engaging with place, memory (forever lost, still in mind, to be recalled), history and time (historiography, decay, narrative), and artifacts (found and collected) when the author's voice was undergoing question and challenge (Who wrote the border ballads? Is this our history? Whom do you trust in their accounting for the past?); when ownership of land and property, and the traditional qualities of the rural and urban environment, were being altered under rational agricultural improvement; when property was being reinvented as landscape; when the status of manufactured goods was changing rapidly in an industrialized northern Europe. Scott's visit to Pompeii, Gell's guiding around the ruins, that dinner with Ritson and the subsequent visit to Gilsland were (re)establishing what constituted an appropriate way of engaging with the past. It is only later on that Scott gets called a romantic historical novelist, Ritson is marginalized as an irascible literary antiquarian, largely forgotten, Gell is seen as a pioneer of topographical survey, and archaeology becomes the rationalized engagement with site and artifact through controlled observation, "fieldwork" and publication in standardized media and genres. This is what I mean when I suggest that insight comes from starting with practices rather than discipline.

In this debate over appropriate ways of engaging with the past, medium is better thought of as mode of engagement—a way of articulating people and artifacts, senses and aspirations, and all the associative chains and genealogical tracks that mistakenly get treated as historical and sociopolitical context. Scott presents us with a fascinating laboratory of such modes of engagement, one that runs from field science to romantic fiction through to what was to be formalized as *Altertumswissenschaft* by German classical philology. By the mid nineteenth century the debate about mediating the past had quieted into an orthodoxy of modes of engagement that came with standardization of practice and publication—an orthodoxy of measurement, inscription and illustration with which we are now very familiar in the *discipline* of Archaeology.

So we have returned to representational media. I suggest that these debates around Scott's and Gell's writing take us deep into contemporary questions regarding the presence of the past. Considerable and growing resources in academic archaeology, museums, and cultural tourism are dedicated today to the delivery of photorealistic reconstruction, to virtual past realities, to visitor experiences that promise to bring the past alive, to museum exhibitions that offer rich multimedia experiences. Wearing a virtual reality visor, watch the ruins of Pompeii rebuild themselves before your very eyes, and share in its ancient inhabitants' return from the dead as animated avatars. Ubiquitous located media offer the opportunity to connect information to place—as you walk along a San Francisco street your mobile media device alerts you that in the building opposite Alfred Hitchcock conceived of his movie *Vertigo*; that before the 1906 earthquake there was a thriving Chinese market right here. Does such technology offer more than Gell's camera lucida and Scott's poetry, Wallis's chorography? The issues and challenges have not changed.

2.9 *Topology and Time*

Figure 10 Howick: The Bathing House. To the left, Molly and Ben inspect microliths eroding from what once was a mesolithic camp, the best preserved in the UK. To the right on the horizon is Dunstanburgh, fortress built by the Earls of Lancaster to rival the royal castle of Bamburgh, to the north. The location was identified in 1808 by Matthew "Monk" Lewis, among others, with Arthurian legend—Sir Guy of the Round Table, "The Seeker," met his supernatural end here. The legend, converted to verse, was recovered by Lewis during a stay with Sir Charles Grey, whose "Bathing House" occupies the center of the photograph. This was built to accommodate Earl and Lady Grey as they watched their many children bathe on the rocky beach, while refreshing themselves with the blend of China tea named after this Prime Minister of England. The addition of the bergamot was reputedly to offset the particular mineral composition of the water on this, their northern family estate of Howick.

Scott's temporal topology intimately connects past and present, manifest in the material connections of land, memories, events, and artifacts, both archaeological remains and media artifacts such as his own poetry and novels. The lack of narrative plot in his poetry and novels is congruent with his focus upon daily life and manners, a vital component of a sense of place in the Borders. The accumulation of details and incidents through people and their times and memories conveys the rich qualities of place. This sense of here-ness, or this-ness, could be called *haecceity*—the distinctive qualities that make a place what it is.

Wallis's archaic chorography was driven by a similar commitment to convey the qualities of a region through reasoned description and commentary, rather than poetry and fiction. The folding of people into the land and its history, human and natural history, is achieved through the device or architecture of the itinerary, the journey through the region. His treatment of what we now call geography was through materials, such as earths and stones, features of the landscape such as geology, weather, rivers and streams, and through plant and animal species. The descriptions he offers, as I illustrated above, focus on qualities of materials, their color, hardness, properties, and, certainly not least, their usefulness (Wallis embraced his contemporary cultural climate of agricultural and industrial improvement). This interest in qualities is what can be called an interest in *quiddity*—the whatness of things that might be described in answer to the question, What are the qualities (of texture, hardness, color, frangibility, etc.) possessed of this thing?

James Hutton's forays into the natural history of the Borders led to quite a different perspective of human history.

Educated in the Humanities, trained as a medic on the Continent, though he never practiced, Hutton first explored the chemical industry, setting up a plant in Edinburgh to manufacture sal-ammoniac from chimney soot. After a couple of successful years, he moved from the city and settled at Slighhouses, a farm belonging to his family, in the fertile Tweed valley near Duns, Berwickshire. Work on improving

Figure 11 Natural History. *Digitalis,* Sycamore Gap, Hadrian's Wall. 2002.

his farms accompanied a keen interest in geology and meteorology as well as plant and animal breeding.

From the 1750s to 1780s he made extensive journeys through much of England and Wales and most regions of Scotland. These were often arduous field trips: "Lord pity the arse that's clagged to a head that will hunt stones" he wrote in a letter to George Clerk Maxwell, August 1774. Hutton agreed that the majority of rocks on the surface of the earth are formed from the debris of former rocks and that the earth's surface is gradually being destroyed by erosion. However, he was the first to connect these phenomena, arguing that the sediments produced by erosion must be consolidated on the seabed and then uplifted to form land—"a new and sublime conclusion" (reported in John Playfair's popularization of Hutton's work in 1802). He believed that heat was the agent of consolidation and uplift and that it also generated, in the interior of the earth, hot fluids from which all crystalline rocks originated. Hutton went further still, claiming that erosion, uplift, and igneous activity were continuous processes which had always, and would always, operate in the same way, and thus that the surface of the earth was continually being recycled, leaving no evidence of how many times this had happened in the past or would happen in the future: the argument for uniformitarianism.

Hutton's fieldwork offered clear evidence of his theories, in geological stratigraphy. On the Berwickshire coast at Siccar Point he found an exposure of sandstone, shales and greywacke, with the strata of the sedimentary rocks lying at an angle to each other (what is now called an unconformity). Another unconformity, inland at Inchbonny by Jedburgh, is now known as the Hutton Unconformity. There was only one way that such configurations could be explained: one layer had been laid down horizontally on the ocean floor, then elevated, folded, and the tops of its folds eroded, subsequently sinking back into the ocean where it formed the base on which the sand was later deposited and consolidated. Such a sequence of events could only have taken place over an immense period of time.

Hutton offered his observations and explanations in a series of publications from the 1780s. He was one of the first to argue for a long chronology for the earth, that what we observe in rock formations indicates its exceptionally ancient age. Indeed Hutton made a radical distinction between human comprehension and what now gets called *deep time*, maintaining that the creation and metamorphosis of the land follows a temporality where, in Hutton's words, "we find no vestige of a beginning, no prospect of an end" (the famous phrase from his *Theory of the Earth*, published in the *Transactions of the Royal Society of Edinburgh* in 1788). The immensity of time and the character of the processes are such that it is time beyond human comprehension, *sublime*. Minds "seemed to grow giddy looking so far into the abyss of time" was the way John Playfair described it (1805, 73).

Hutton also applied these uniformitarian arguments to life forms, the basis of evolutionary process. This came as part of a three volume work *An Investigation of the Principles of Knowledge and the Progress of Reason, from Sense to Science and Philosophy*, 1794. Having stated that the true merit of scientific investigation lies in providing the facts on which to base a sound guide to conduct and belief, Hutton presented a complete metaphysical system partly derived from Locke, Berkeley, and Hume. Again, experimental reason is treated as complementary

Figure 12 Binchester Roman Fort. Excavations along Dere Street, 2010.

to speculative philosophy and ethics. Causation is a major topic, but he also dealt with time, space, religion, morality, politics, and education.

Above, in connection with experiences of decay and death, I introduced the concept of the abject. Here it is again. Hutton's time without limits, visible in the folding of a stratigraphic unconformity, is a different quality of time to the human histories folded into the landscape. Observations on the stratigraphy of rocks take us to the edge of an abyss of time, deep time beyond human comprehension. The abject here is *the sublime,* a kind of experience that takes us over the edge, that is rooted in what cannot be contained, that exceeds any category intended to capture its essence. The sublime was a key aspect of the landscape aesthetics of the eighteenth century: the experience of vast empty mountain ranges, of waterfalls and rapids, of landscapes that defy description of their physical qualities, that exceed the enumeration of their features.

We are surely dealing here with one of the most evocative components of an archaeological sensibility—awareness of the immediacy, the presence of the *deep* past. It is captured in the archetype of the fingerprint on a pot. We can touch the (momentary) past, intimately human, across aeons of time. I find so evocative and stirring the sixty-nine footprints, now fossilized and discovered in 1978, left on a riverbank at Laetoli in east Africa by a family group of members of the species *Australopithecus Afarensis* 3.6 million years ago:

> The footprint trail ... shows a steady progression from south to north of two hominids, perhaps walking side by side. One set of prints is large, the other small. Were they male and female? Were the smaller prints made by a child? Part way along the trail, the hominids appear to have paused, turned, and looked westward. What caught their attention? The answer is lost in time, but after the pause they resumed walking in the original direction—as if they knew exactly where they were going. (Johanson and Edgar 1996, 132)

2.10 *Collectors and Conservators*

I hadn't really come to understand much of Scott until I visited his house, Abbotsford. Scott had lived with family, rented and leased for forty years until 1811, when, as a successful author, he bought Clarty Hole (muddy hole), just on the Scottish side of the Borders, and set about converting the farmhouse into a remarkable Gothic memory palace. Renamed Abbotsford, the house looks south towards England over the River Tweed that runs at the end of the garden terrace, the river that forms the borderline along its lower course towards the coast at Berwick.

Figure 13 Abbotsford. Scottish Borders. Entrance Hall, looking towards the Study. 2008.

The Entrance Hall is theatrical, a stage set, what now seems like a caricature, with carved oak paneling, suits of armor flanking the doors, and the skull of Scottish hero Robert the Bruce on the mantelpiece of the massive stone fireplace. The fruits of Scott's excavations of the battlefield of Waterloo hang on the walls—cuirasses, some with bullet holes, helmets, lances, swords. To the left, now in a vitrine, is a silver urn given to Scott by Byron, and containing the bones of "Attic heroes" from the battle of Marathon. Around the corridor the keys to Lochleven castle hang on the wall; Douglas used them to help the escape of Mary Queen of Scots in 1568. Behind them is Rob Roy's claymore and dirk in this armory leading to the Drawing Room and Library, with its claustrophobic, book-lined, windowless Study connecting back to the Entrance Hall.

Scott wasn't satisfied with the first wing added to the old farmhouse, in the currently fashionable "modern Gothic—a style I hold to be equally false and foolish." He decided "to Scottify it" with detailing from old Scots precedents. This was extended to most of the additions. Fragments of celebrated historic buildings, bits of old Edinburgh and local ruined abbeys were bought up and incorporated into Abbotsford. Ruskin later complained of the new setting for the door of the old Edinburgh tolbooth; it was demolished in 1817 along with a lot more of the city as Edinburgh became the "Athens of the North." As well as original fragments, plaster casts were used to add authentic, if not original, details. The stair turret brings to mind many others on Scottish towers. The crosses on the gables reference Melrose Abbey. And there is plenty of crennellation and ranks of chimneys along the rooftops.

Abbotford appears a staged, though private world, because it is so carefully composed, and because it is the site, so clearly, where Scott worked and wrote (the library and study are so prominent), where he entertained, showing off this home for his collections. It is difficult to appreciate its originality and impact, because so much has become so familiar and hackneyed, just as the plots of Scott's novels have provided the basis for popular adventure over the last two centuries, from melodrama to Hollywood, just as Scotland has become identified, for better or worse, with so many of the stories recounted by Scott in the likes of his *Tales of a Grandfather.* For Clive Wainwright, Abbotsford is the paradigm of *The Romantic Interior, The British Collector at Home, 1750–1850,* the title of his book published in 1989. With its quotations and references, its replication and pastiche, original and reconstructed, it is the objective architectural correlative of the antiquarian imagination.

John Clayton's correlative was the landscape itself. To the south of Abbotsford and overlooking the river Tyne is Chesters, his home from 1796 till his death in 1890. Clayton, Town Clerk for forty-five years, was a key figure in the redevelopment of the booming local industrial city of Newcastle. He was instrumental in helping realize the visionary designs of Richard Grainger for a neo-Classical city center, one of the first planned commercial urban centers in Europe. At home he was a passionate antiquarian. Hadrian's Wall runs through the estate he grew up on and inherited. In the landscaped fields next to the house are the remains of Cilurnum, the fort on the Wall that guarded the river crossing. From the 1840s Clayton began excavating, and continued intermittently for nearly half a century. What marks out Clayton as extraordinary, however, is his attitude towards the preservation of historic landscapes. From the 1830s Clayton used his wealth to buy up parts of Hadrian's Wall and the surrounding land, so as to be able to stop the dilapidation and destruction of the Wall through neglect, but more from the deliberate removal of the stone for building and field boundaries. He followed purchase with excavation and consolidation, and then opened up to tourism much of the spectacular central section, as it traverses the cliffs of the Whin Sill across a wild moorland landscape. This was the modern beginnings of cultural resource management.

The Duke and Duchess of Northumberland, mentioned in my discussion of Thomas Percy's *Reliques of Ancient English Poetry,* enthusiastically embraced their new titles, reestablished in 1766, and decided to restore the ancient border fortress of Alnwick, their seat in Northumberland. The grounds were landscaped by local Lancelot "Capability" Brown in modern parkland fashion; the walls and keep were renovated and Robert Adam designed new gothic interiors. The town was given a complete makeover and improved with fine stone houses and a market building, a gothic bridge and a lion atop a column. This is what Lady Holland said about the castle in 1798:

> Alnwick, on the outside, revives the recollection of all one has heard of baronial splendour, battlements, towers, gateways, portcullis, etc., immense courts, thick walls, and everything demonstrative of savage solitary, brutal power and magnitude. The late Duchess built the present fabric upon the site of the primitive castle, but much is from a traditional guess. The inside corresponds but feebly with the outward promise; the whole is fitted up in a tinsel, gingerbread taste rather adapted to a theatrical representation. (Quoted by Hines, 1999, 123)

This is exactly the modern baronial gothic that Scott despised. And though the interiors were redone by the Fourth Duke in the 1850s, Alnwick has remained enough of a theater setting to serve in several movies, one of the most recent being as Harry Potter's Hogwarts.

As well as a matter of taste, authenticity was certainly in question. Richard Davenport Hines picks this up in his racy book *Gothic: Four Hundred Years of Excess, Horror, Evil and Ruin* (1999). The pretensions of the Duke and Duchess to be authentic members of the Percy family, in whose line had run the title Northumberland, were much mocked. "That great vulgar Countess has been laid up with a hurt on her leg," Horace Walpole gossiped in 1759:

> The Duchess of Grafton asked if it were true that Lady Rebecca Poulett kicked her?—'Kicked me madam! When did you ever hear of a Percy that took a kick?' ... Lord March making them a visit this summer at Alnwick Castle, my Lord received him at the gate, and said, 'I believe, my Lord, this is the first time that ever a Douglas and a Percy met here in friendship'—think of this from a Smithson to a true Douglas. (Quoted by Hines, 1999, 123)

Sir Charles Monck decided *not* to restore his family castle of Belsay in the south east of Northumberland. This very fine fourteenth century tower was extended with a Jacobean wing after the union of the crowns in the early seventeenth century and was the home of the Middleton family. Monck inherited it in 1795, together with another estate, from his maternal grandfather (which prompted his change of name from Middleton to Monck). In 1804 he set off on a two year honeymoon that included a tour through Germany and a long stay in Greece. He had had a traditional classical education at Rugby School and clearly got caught up in the current enthusiasm for all things ancient and Greek: he sketched various new neo-Classical buildings in Germany, and in Athens fell in with William Gell at the time of the publication of his *Topography of Troy* and when he was working on what was to be his *Itinerary of Greece*. The experience was revelatory: on his return to Belsay Monck set about designing a new house inspired by his first hand experience of Classical Greek architecture. Ten years of building produced one of the most consistent applications of contemporary understanding of the geometry of ancient Greek architecture to a modern residence.

The two hundred and more drawings for the project that still remain—the plans and ideas that lay behind the house—show that this was very much a personal project. One architectural drawing for the hall was by Gell, though Monck's zeal for accuracy led to something quite different from the optical consistency I have discussed in Gell's topography. The theme is the Doric order, very much interpreted in what is almost a meditation on proportion and geometry. The house is exactly one hundred feet square. Exactly—Monck insisted that the proportional ratios of the design be calculated to three decimal places, forcing masons to abandon their conventional measurements in eighths of an inch. There are few direct quotations from the original Greek, though the Tower of the Winds in Athens appears at Belsay as the octagonal lantern on the stables. This is more a rationalist reworking of what people like Monck and Gell (and William Wilkins, another antiquary and architect friend) thought that Greek architecture represented. The fronts of the house are exceptionally severe, wholly plain apart from the fluted Doric columns at the entrance and the pilasters: the emphasis is simply on proportion, line and surface; the roof was low-pitched so as to be invisible from ground level, kept from intruding upon the rectangular geometry. There is

Figure 14 Belsay Castle. Northumberland, 2001.

even evidence that the library bookcases echo the proportions of the Erechtheion on the Acropolis in Athens, as measured by Monck.

The nearby village was demolished and the site turned over to a quarry for building stone; the locals were rehoused in a model village on the main road between Newcastle and Jedburgh. Monck abandoned the castle and old house, turning them into a ruin. The quarry was then converted into a garden, connecting the new house with the ruin: it looks like a painting by Salvator Rosa, on the wild side of the picturesque—tumble-down grottoes, seating niches by springs in the rock faces, a look of natural abandon in the ferns and undergrowth, punctuated by exotic imported rhododendra. Formal gardens immediately around the house become parkland in the manner of Capability Brown and Repton, as at Alnwick, with much use of walls concealed in trenches (ha-ha walls) that open up views across the estate and to the hillside opposite, forested with unusual conifers, Scots Pine and native hardwoods. Monck's variation on the Theseion in Athens, his own temple to rational system, was a focus of human order in a landscape that was less cultivated and more suggestive of chaos and decay the further it was from the house, just as the modern finds new life in the ancient, and the ruin of history becomes a charming after-dinner walk through the picturesque.

The theme in the archaeological imagination given different inflection in these building projects is one of the possibility, feasibility and, crucially, the desirability of rebuilding the past, making good the loss of time and ruin. A key archaeological task is to sort through the debris of history. And then what? To witness the loss by consolidating ruins as just that, ruins in a new landscape? To rebuild and restore, to fill in the gaps? To replicate exactly? Or to build again, incorporating the past into the present? Does authenticity lie in the original fragment, the broken stone statue itself, or in the principles of proportion and order of an ancient culture? Or even in a sentiment such as baronial splendor?

In his book *The Past is a Foreign Country* (1985), David Lowenthal reminds us of this ambivalent, even paradoxical, attitude towards antiquity held since the Renaissance humanists. After Petrarch, retrieving antiquity could be seen as a necromancy of rebirth, reincarnation, even resurrection. Working on ancient texts was conceived in explicitly archaeological terms—unearthing fragments (see Alain Schnapp's *Discovery of the Past* [1996] for many variations on this elision). And the ruins of classical antiquity, the exhumed and lacerated relics, buildings, artifacts, texts, needed reconstruction. They needed a creative rebirth that came through their inclusion in the present, their metamorphosis into new work, the dead restored to life and health. Early scientists could describe their work as the restoration of ancient wisdom because innovation and renovation were the same.

To invent was not to devise a solution unknown to previous generations, but to find something which had been lost—in Latin, *invenire* is to uncover or come upon. The paradox is that, in order to preserve the past, it must be creatively reused, even destroyed. And herein lies an archaeological anxiety, that in order to know the past, we dig, we intervene and destroy.

The Revs Program at Stanford (revs.stanford.edu) was established in 2011 to study the history of cars and automobility, to bring a human and historical perspective to bear upon our understanding of automobile design and people's relationships with an iconic component of modernity in an archaeology of the contemporary past. We are working upon a collection of cars, with an archive of texts and imagery, with a community of enthusiasts passionate about what is so much more than an industrial artifact. One set of answers to the question we are posing of what can be done with old cars concerns collection and restoration. How should an old car be restored, to prevent it from rusting and rotting? Bruce Canepa Design is a restoration studio and museum in nearby Scotts Valley. Bruce's displayed vehicles are absolutely and remarkably pristine. His team can restore a car to as-new condition, stripping back to bare metalwork and completely rebuilding. You can step back in time as you open the door of the black Mark II Jaguar I encountered in his workshop, back to when the car was on the showroom floor in 1965. But the Jaguar has no life, I feel. Miles Collier's 1933 Bentley, once owned by Yorkshireman Eddie Hall, still has the rear light roughly mounted to illuminate the number decal required to race at LeMans in 1950. The original cracked leather seating, on which Eddie sat in that race, is there, too, and the instruments on the dash are clean and perfectly functioning but marked by the patina of age and use. Signs of wear are marks of life that lend character to the car's physiognomy; they witness the life of the artifact and its relationships with its drivers, passengers, the travels it has traced. Relevant concepts here are originality and authenticity, the genuine and the fake, maintenance, conservation and restoration. All revolve around a fundamental disposition we find in an archaeological sensibility—a *care* for things.

In a classic case of archaeological restoration, Arthur Evans cared deeply about the site he was excavating —Knossos, a prehistoric architectural complex on the Aegean island of Crete. The winter rains that fell after the first summer seasons of excavation in the 1900s starting dissolving away the excavated ruins. He had roofs erected, and then took a remarkably daring step of rebuilding Knossos in iron, concrete and plaster, not so much as it had been, but as a restored ruin that very much witnesses Evans's own archaeological vision of this prehistoric culture located somewhere between Edwardian and Art Deco England. This has been very controversial. Just where in history is this Knossos? How representative of the original are the restorations? Some, and I am with them, consider that Evans created a Knossos between past and present, not least by building a simulacrum of ruin: the restorations look like ruins, but are not (though they are now in the process themselves of restoration as water seepage has rusted the iron frameworks and cracked the concrete). In this the ruins of Knossos are genuine, because they generate response that makes us so conscious precisely of the challenges faced when we care for the past. Immortality is not an option. We must accept loss and decay, though we may choose to care and work upon the remains.

3. An Archaeological Narratology

My nine and more vignettes from the Borders in the eighteenth and early nineteenth centuries have introduced a host of connected concerns in the modern archaeological imagination: artifacts and accounts, the different kinds of connection between past and present, senses of history and change, locality and belonging, and the ruin of time and change. A complementary richness can be found in the miscellany of literary reflections on history, heritage and the past gathered by David Lowenthal in his classic *The Past is a Foreign Country* (1987). Jennifer Wallace has sensitively explored treatments of excavation, death, and the sepulchral in an eclectic selection of literature and writing mainly from the English romantic tradition and the nineteenth century (*Digging the Dirt: The Archaeological Imagination*, 2004). These two authors break down the archaeological imagination according to themes.

Under her guiding topic of "digging," Jennifer Wallace finds the following themes in the poems and literature she studied:

The Archaeological Imagination by Michael Shanks, 127–144.

- Stones in the landscape
- Bodies unearthed
- Excavation and desire
- Seeking epic origins (Troy)
- Digging into despair
- Holy ground
- Landfill and garbage.

David Lowenthal's perspective is broader, encompassing the reception of the past. Here are his themes:

- Revisiting and reliving the past: dreams and nightmares
- Benefits and burdens of the past
- Ancients and Moderns: tradition and innovation
- The look of age: decay and wear
- Knowing the past: experience and belief, history and memory
- Changing the past: display, protection, reenactment, commemoration
- Creative anachronism: contemporary pasts.

Wallace's and Lowenthal's thematics are very useful, and offer frames for their wonderful observations, glosses and insights. They are nonetheless somewhat loose, inductive and descriptive, and offer little analysis of why the archaeological imagination presents itself in the way it does.

Is it possible to go further and parse the archaeological imagination, break it down analytically into constituent processes? Does it have a grammar or logic? In my book *Experiencing the Past* I attempted to parse a generic archaeological encounter with the past, and presented a somewhat abstract and formal model of the components of archaeological work or craft in general, what goes on when an archaeologist gets to work on remains. I kept the model open to metaphorical elaboration: as Lowenthal and Wallace have so well illustrated, metaphor is indeed a means by which the archaeological imagination works. The titles of both of their books refer to this: "digging deep" and another spatial metaphor—the past as "a foreign country."

Let me suggest another approach. I have deliberately sketched scenarios, characters, settings, motivations, plots and performances. Much of the archaeological imagination has to do with the way we might make sense of our relationships with the past, its remains, traditions, and their relationship to our senses of self and identity. Let's follow Scott and treat the archaeological imagination as a field of stories and allegories about ourselves and the roles we play in history and in recalling the past. I will offer a semiotic reading of the stories I have told of antiquarians in the Borders. To be more precise, I adopt that approach broadly called narratology, analysis of the grammar of narratives, the structure that underlies different particular stories, here of the past and what antiquarians and archaeologists do.

This is nothing particularly new in archaeology. The anthropological turn in archaeology in the 1970s and 1980s involved, among other things, treating culture as communication, as a semiotic field, treating artifacts as signs and signifiers, component parts of systems of meaning that make sense of the world. Chris Tilley and I, for example, showed how the way people treated remains of the dead in early farming communities in Britain and Sweden, in earthen long barrows and megalithic monuments, communicated a certain representation of the way their society worked and saw itself. This appeared in our contribution to a collection of studies edited by Ian Hodder in 1982 under the title *Symbolic and Structural Archaeology*. It is not difficult to find in basic archaeology textbooks a good account of this "linguistic turn" through to interpretive theory and method (what is still often called, opaquely, *postprocessual* archaeology). There are also much older traditions of interpreting meaning in those archaeologies informed by art history: iconography and iconology are well-established methodologies for establishing the identity of two and three dimensional representations. In my research on ancient Greek Corinthian pottery, for example, comparing and contrasting the figures in painted friezes, looking at the details and the patterns of association, could lead to secure identification of particular characters and even stories: Herakles and his bow, Zeus and his thunderbolt, Bellerophon fighting the

Chimaera. The key to all these approaches to understanding the design of cultural artifacts is establishing patterns of association and contrast, whether in the treatment of bones, or in painted pictures of people and animals. Let's turn such attention to archaeology itself. What of the practices of antiquarians and archaeologists? What of the *meanings and significances* of what they do and how they describe themselves and their encounters with the past?

One starting point is narratology, the theory and study of narrative and narrative structure. Let me briefly rehearse the background and features. In his tour de force of 1928, *Morphology of the Folktale,* Vladimir Propp extended Russian formalist linguistic and literary analysis to folk tales. He broke down a large number of Russian folk tales into their smallest structural (formal) components, and, on the basis of common factors, developed a typology of narrative structures, the building blocks from which the folk tales were constructed. These included eight character types (such as villain, dispatcher, hero) and thirty-one functions or plot permutations (such as leaving home, warning, unrecognized return). (There's a fascinating web site that allows you to design your own fairy tale using Propp's system—http://www.stonedragonpress.com/vladimir_propp/propp_generator_v1.htm.) The key point is that form and structure matter as much as content.

Hayden White's *Metahistory: The Historical Imagination in Nineteenth-Century Europe* (1973) applied this premise to the writing of historical narrative. The argument is that history is as much about historiography, writing history, as it is about historical sources and events. And historiography relies substantially on forms of narrative. So Hayden's topic was the logic and rhetoric of historiography. In his study of several nineteenth century historians (including Carlyle, Michelet, Ranke), he identified the major permutations in how they constructed history through narrative, different combinations of rhetorical stance, emplotment, argument, and ideology. He extended four key rhetorical tropes (figures of speech/style—metaphor, metonymy, synecdoche, irony) into forms of discourse—that is, deep generative historiographical structures. Again, the project was to reunite historical studies with literature and the humanities in attending to the constitutive imagination of the historian in representing sources and events. Plot and the other components of narrative are not only a structural component of fictional or mythical stories; they are crucial to the historical representations of events as well.

I repeat that the key to all these approaches to understanding the design of cultural artifacts is establishing patterns of association and contrast. Ferdinand de Saussure's insight that meaning depends upon difference, and particularly systems of difference, has had considerable influence (the word "cat" has no intrinsic relationship to the furry creature and only carries meaning because it is different from the word "dog") (see Culler 1976 for an introduction). It is the cornerstone of structuralist, and indeed post-structuralist, method, from the Prague linguistic Circle of the 1930s, most notably Roman Jakobson and Nikolai Trubetzkoy, through Claude Levi-Strauss to Jacques Derrida. And in such systems of difference, binary opposition plays a major role. In that study of neolithic mortuary practices just mentioned, Tilley and I offered oppositions such as skeleton:bones, flesh and blood:dry remains, dark chamber:light exterior, individual:community, as the architecture of analysis. It is not difficult to appreciate how our contemporary academic disciplines take many such binary oppositions as a premise: sciences:arts, nature:culture, structure:action, theory:practice. All social and cultural theory involves taking a stand on these "Cartesian dualisms." Tilley and I, in our project of the 1980s, made much of the need to negotiate and overcome these dualisms in an archaeology that bridged disciplines, with our archaeological object being peoples' past lives, human nature and culture in material and imagined worlds (Shanks and Tilley 1987a and 1987b). More recently Julian Thomas has convincingly shown in his book *Archaeology and Modernity* (2004) how binary oppositions structure the whole history of archaeological thinking since the eighteenth century. *Archaeology: the Discipline of Things* (Bjørnar Olsen, Michael Shanks, Tim Webmoor and Chris Witmore 2012) outlines the history of the particular opposition between people and things as it is played out in disciplinary forms of archaeological practice, subsuming both within different forms of engagement between past and present such as survey, excavation, classification, modeling and visualization.

In *Three Landscapes,* an interdisciplinary project that ran at Stanford Humanities Center in 2000–2001, an artist (architect, dramaturge and scenographer Cliff McLucas), a theologian (the Jesuit Dorian Llywelyn), and an archaeologist (myself) took as a topic three particular (historical) landscapes: the seismological in California, the archaeological in Sicily, and the sublime in Wales. Landscape is one of those hybrid concepts that belie easy categorization. Landscape refers to both human perception and experience of the land, cultural and social forms of inhabitation as well as topography and physical geography. The term is difficult to separate from a complex ideological history in western representations of human inhabitation as well as of landed property: landscape is a term in the fine arts and beyond at the heart of notions of the picturesque and sublime. Our purpose was to unpack these complexities in an exploration of representational practices (the academic essay, performed lecture, graphical layout, cartography) that would allow the tensions in the concept to open up the richness of human engagements with land and environment, rather than close them down. The triangulation of three case studies was designed to help break up the binary terms behind landscape. Coming from three very different backgrounds, we aimed to overcome disciplinary boundaries in a common focus upon a complex (non-disciplinary) object—landscape. In our work on accounts of Californian geology (most notably the fault lines), (pre)historic landscapes of western Sicily (under archaeological investigation), and the eighteenth century landed estate of Thomas Johnes at Hafod in west Wales (newly conserved in the 1990s), we encountered the need to analyze, to compare and contrast very different kinds of narratives and stories of land.

At a colloquium we attended on the topic of Narrative, a paper by Ewa Domanska came as a revelation. Ewa is a philosopher of historiography at the Adam Mickiewicz University in Poznan. The talk we heard at Stanford was called "Six Theses on Archaeology-to-come." The argument was that the logical/formal structure of archaeological engagements with remains of the past indicates that archaeology is actually a specific way of thinking through things that are future oriented. This is, of course, counter intuitive: typically archaeology is associated with study of the past. But just consider how archaeology can only act upon the past as a contemporary (and therefore future-oriented) *project* that aims to recover, conserve, preserve what is in the process of being lost through decay, neglect or whatever. Ewa grounded her argument in a schematic that can be used to see into the working of binary oppositions. She used the semiotic square, a graphical formalization of concepts associated with Algirdas Julien Greimas (Greimas and Rastier 1968, Greimas 1983, see Lenoir 1994).

Here is her diagram (figure 15).

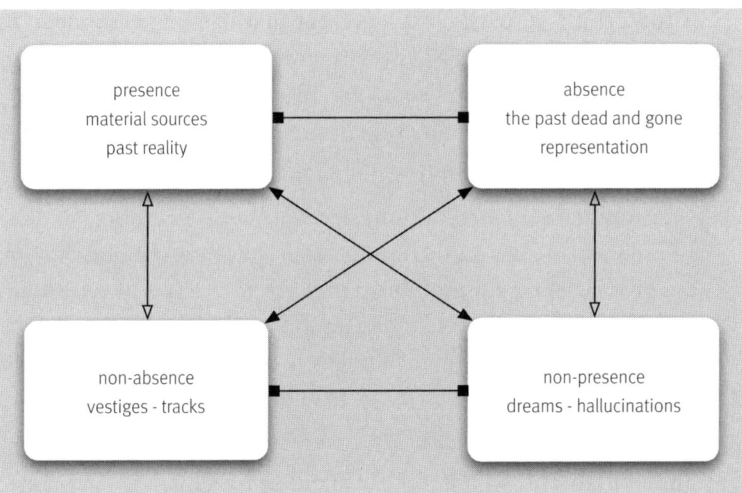

Figure 15 Phantasmatic reality.

Begin with a pair of opposites: the remains of the past in the *present,* and the *absent* past to which they refer; call them positive and negative terms. Add to these their contradictions, the non-present (a negation of the positive) and the non-absent (a negation of the negative). Consider what these different terms are in relation to each other. The absent past may imply that it is non-present, but these are *not* the same thing. The material reality of the past, the primary positive term in the diagram, consists of remains or traces in the present. The absent past to which they refer takes the form, typically, of the representations of the past that we construct on the basis of these traces; these might be catalogs and descriptions of the remains, or models and narratives. In contradiction to material traces are non-present forms or hallucinations that have no material reality or basis; clearly these are not the same as representations of the past, though they may appear to be. Ewa made much of the fourth term, the contradiction of an absent represented past, the non-absent past, implied by presence, but not the same. As she put it, "The problem with the past is not that it is absent or non-present, but that it is non-absent" (Domanska, personal communication). What is this? How can the past be non-absent?

A footprint is a mark on the present that has lingered, made in the past. The non-absent past is the impression made by the past on the present: the Latin term is *vestigium*, vestige; in Greek *ichnos*, track. The non-absent past is actually very familiar; it is the past that comes back to haunt. It is Freud's notion of the uncanny:

> Uncanny is in reality nothing foreign, but something familiar and old-established in the mind that has been estranged only by the process of repression. This reference to the fact of repression enables us furthermore to understand Schelling's definition of the uncanny as something which ought to have been kept concealed but which has nevertheless come to light. (*Freud, 2003 [1919], 148,* translation amended)

The non-absent is ghost-like, a sign left by somebody or something that was once present, but has passed and is gone, lost: a phantasm. For Ewa, this phantasmatic reality is one rooted in future legacy. The footprint or vestige is not like a trace, a material presence; it *will* haunt, when it is found in the future and then witnesses the passing over of what is no more. Its time or temporality, therefore, is neither purely of the past nor the present, nor the re-presented past; it is the past-as-it-interrupts-the-present. The Greek term for such time is *kairos*—the moment of discovery or opportunity, when the

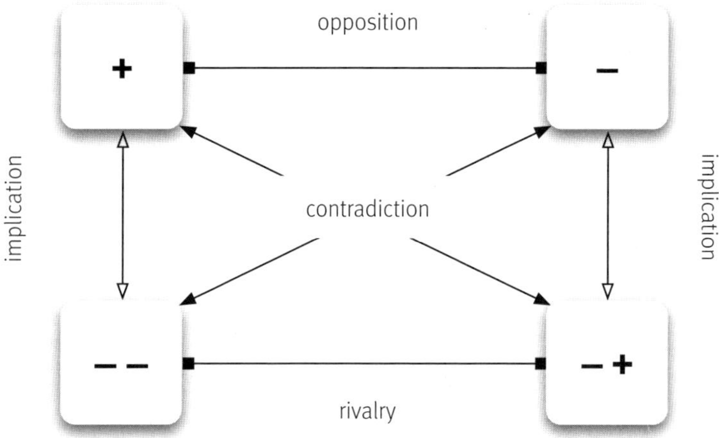

Figure 16 The semiotic square.

past flashes up in the present and prompts reaction. Another term for this kind of time is *actuality*.

A semiotic square (figure 16) is a visual representation of the logical articulation of any category. You start with a term, category, theme that is important to a narrative, scenario or account and then map various types of oppositions and relationships:

- antonyms or contrasts (logical "contraries"): terms which are comparatively graded on the same implicit dimension (for example, good:bad, where "not good" is not necessarily "bad"; in Ewa's analysis the terms were presence and absence);
- oppositions (logical "contradictories"): mutually exclusive terms (for example alive:not alive);
- implications: terms that may appear synonymous, but actually can be distinguished through their relationship with contrary and contradictory terms (as in the example just given: a trace is not a vestige; the non-absent past [vestige] is implied by the notion of a present past [trace], but is not the same when you consider how it is in contradiction to an absent past, and is contrary to a hallucination or non-present past).

The distinction between contrasts and oppositions, contraries and contradictories is basically one between digital and analogue relationships—analogue distinctions or contrasts are more-or-less; digital differences or contradictions are either:or.

Greimas developed the semiotic square partly as a tool of narratology, to visualize the different formal components of a narrative on the basis of a chosen term and its binary relationships. Ewa's particular square is an application to the stories that can be told about encounters with the remains of the past. The power of the schematic is heuristic: the diagram opens up the narratological field, suggesting possibilities, revealing features missed by a more cursory inspection. While an orthodox account of archaeology may center upon material traces, discovered remains of the past, such a narratological diagram suggests other components and significances, here connecting traces with haunting ghosts and footprints, and identifying aspects of their ontology and temporality.

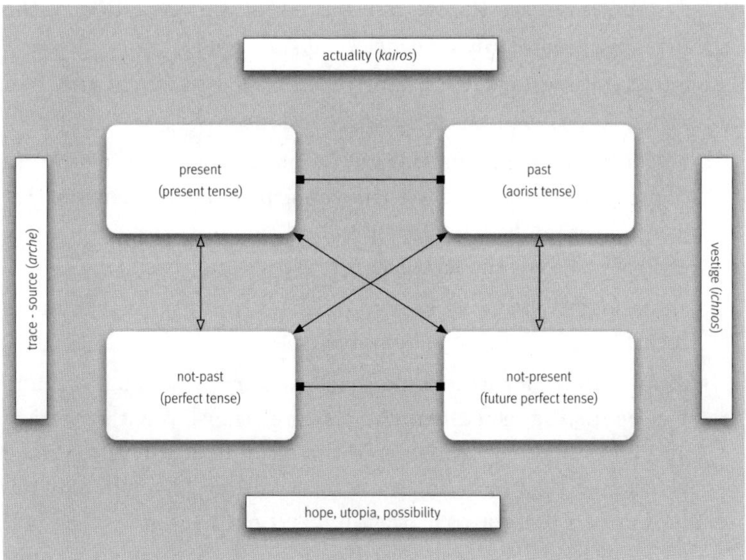

Figure 17 Memory and redemption.

Back now to the archaeological imagination in the Borders. I am going to present a series of semiotic squares. They connect and overlap, as a term in one is taken up in another; in technical terms they can be taken to form syntagmatic chains and paradigmatic harmonies. The purpose, to repeat, is heuristic, to map out the different components of the archaeological imagination.

So let's continue with the contrast between the trace and the vestige and clarify these aspects of archaeological time.

Setting the present in opposition to the past, as times or tenses, invokes the corresponding contradictory temporal states: the past that still has an effect on the present (they have done this), and the past to be (they will have done this). The diagram in figure 17 delivers four temporal states of being in the archaeological imagination: trace and vestige, which we have already seen; actuality (the Greek *kairos*), or the moment of intervention of past in the present, for example in its discovery; hope and future prospect. This dynamic is captured in the call from Adorno and Horkheimer in their *Dialectic of Enlightenment* (1941)—"What is needed is not the preservation of the past, but the redemption of past hopes"—a particular kind of political representation.

"Sleeps the sweet voice of Cona, in the midst of his rustling hall?" (Ossian, quoted above). One aspect of (past) presence invoked in so many of the antiquarian debates of the eighteenth century is voice (figure 18). Add its contrary, silence, and the contradictions of noise that carries no meaning, and sound that may be a voice, and we have four modes of attention, listening and making sense: speech—direct conveyance of meaning; ambient noise (and silence) against which we hear and distinguish meaning; decoding a signal in that ambient noise; translating one language into another. This diagram indicates, I suggest, the importance in the archaeological imagination of the necessity to decode and translate, not least in source criticism and commentary, and also that there is no sense without the everyday mundane background of human life, against which meaningful work and historical events happen.

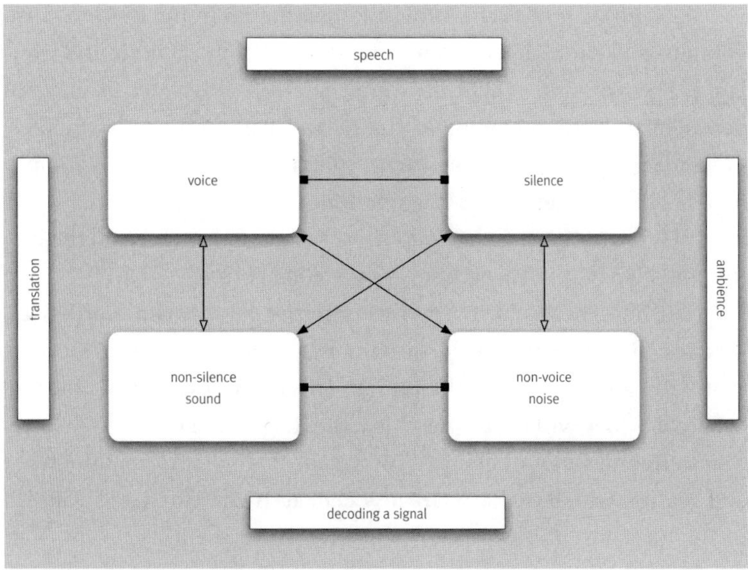

Figure 18 The voice against the wind.

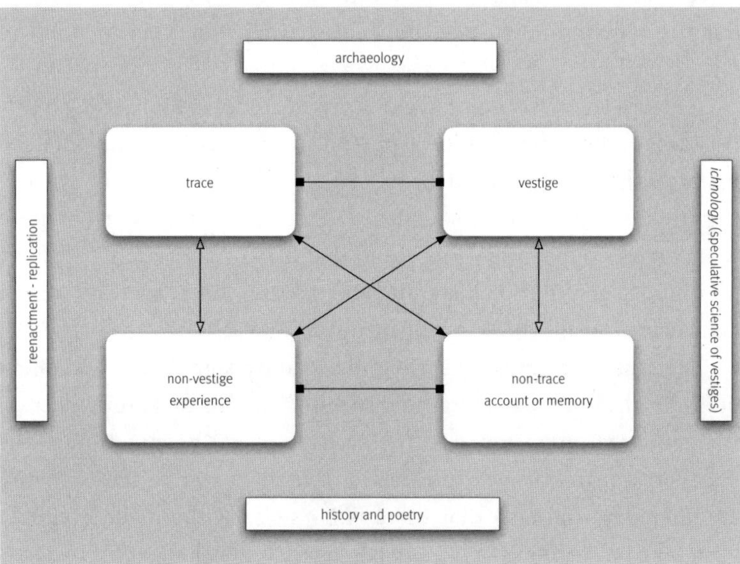

Figure 19 The Antiquarian's choice.

If trace and vestige are opposed directly (figure 19), we are offered various options in applying the archaeological imagination in reconstructing the past. Archaeology typically involves both traces and vestiges. *Ichnology* works with vestiges and mediations (accounts or memories); it is of necessity speculative (in Hume's sense discussed above) in having to make up for absences. Documentary sources (non-traces) combine with human experience in history, and poetry: consider the importance, emphasized by Hayden White, of narrative form to both historiography and fiction. The challenge is to reanimate the past by describing and accounting for experiences that resonate and make sense to people today. Animating fragments of the past can be said to occur, for example, when archaeologists replicate past processes, of manufacture and of human experience, through objects themselves (and this includes experimental archaeology).

A primary subject of figure 20 is the work of the collector-connoisseur, distinguishing authentic from fake. This is a process

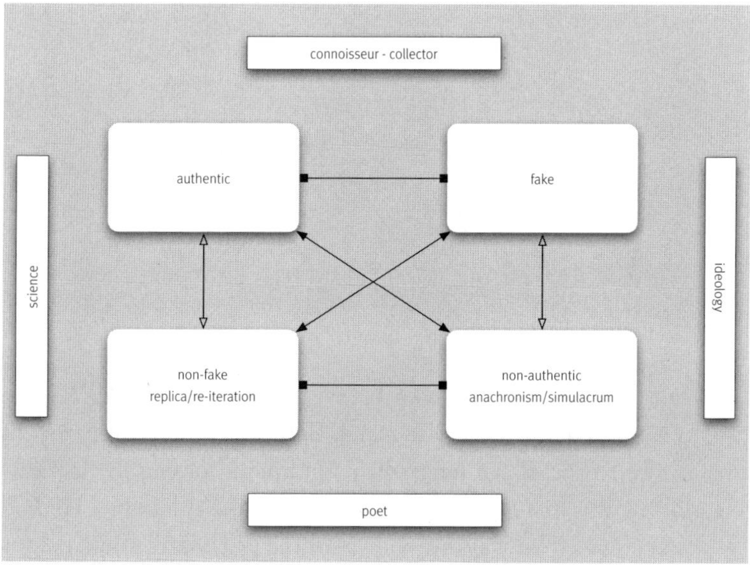

Figure 20 The necessity of critique.

revealed to be intimately connected with the creativity of the poet, and bridging science and ideology, when the two contradictories are included. This is because an authentic, non-fake past need not be original: it may be a replica or model that captures more or less of the past. Correspondingly, anachronisms connect past and present, but fail to adequately respect the past with an ideological imposition of present views and notions; the simulacrum, to follow Baudrillard's usage, is the non-authentic fake, the exact copy of an original that never existed. A creative appropriation of the past may be to negotiate between the replica and the simulacrum, as indeed in Scott's poetry and novels.

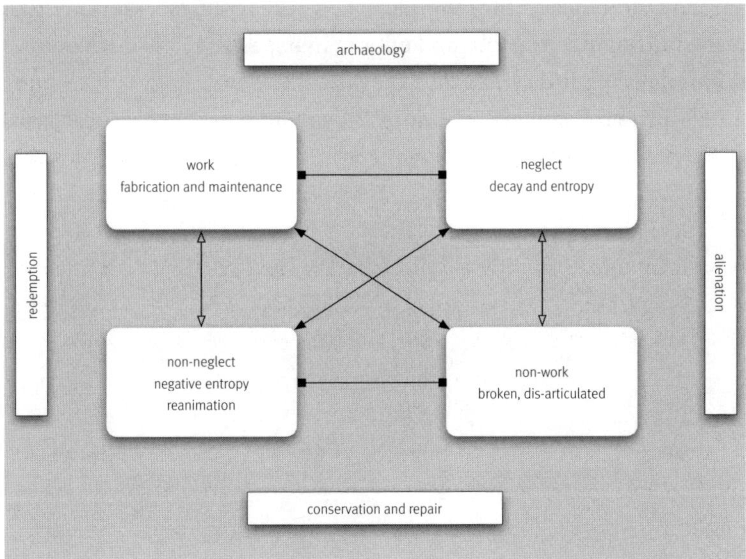

Figure 21 The craft of archaeology.

In Naples, Scott wasn't interested in the antiquities of Pompeii, but, in the words of his biographer, set about "feverishly" collecting old manuscripts and working on a novel about bandits. He *had* to be busy, not looking at the ruins with the eye of an antiquary, but working as a poet. The site of Pompeii was disappointment and anathema, a dead ruin. The work of an archaeologist can be described as maintaining links between the past and the present through the fabrication of trenches in the ground, museums, academic papers, etc. The contrary here is neglect of the past that leads to decay and entropy, natural processes. Ruins and remains that are left to themselves are a broken past, disarticulated, and alienated from the present. The application of archaeological work can reanimate the past and reverse the entropy. Again, this is "redemptive" work (figure 17).

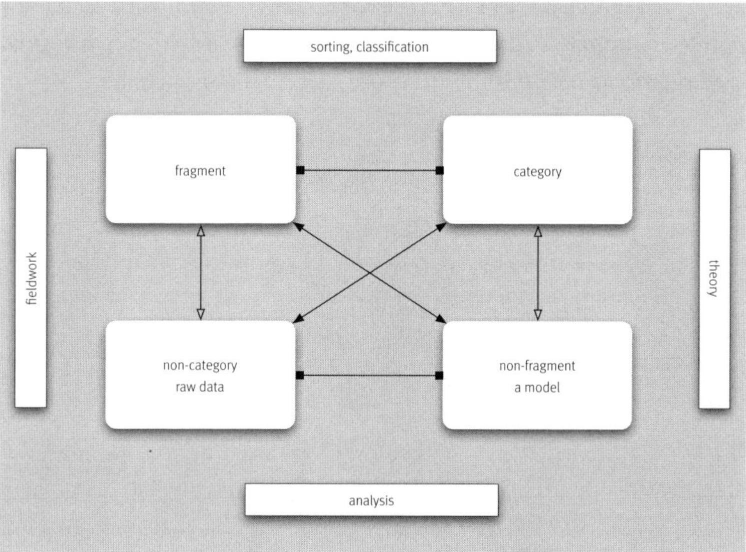

Figure 22 Potsherds, tables and boxes.

A more abstract title for figure 22 could be "The real and the conjectural." Fragments of the past, such as potsherds, are sorted according to categories: this is the primary opposition in the diagram: the real and the tool of thought. The potsherds are always more than the categories or boxes that hold them: raw data always overflow the simplification that turns them into (categorized) information that can be used in analysis. (They don't fit, and as such, are abject.) Non-categorized data, indeed, the bits of the past coming out of fieldwork, must be turned into information to be useful. On their own, categories, the key component of classification, need to be more than just boxes to put things in: a model or narrative is needed to hold them together and make sense of them. This always involves theory and, again in Hume's usage, conjecture. Theory and modeling fill in the gaps. It is not inappropriate again to think of this as embodied practice: the archaeologist may sort the potsherds by putting them in different boxes on different tables, representing, perhaps, different periods and styles. In the museum the fragments are arranged in cases or vitrines to order and to tell a story or make a point. It was in that shrine of an antiquarian's study that Scott gathered the manuscripts and sources to turn them into a ballad.

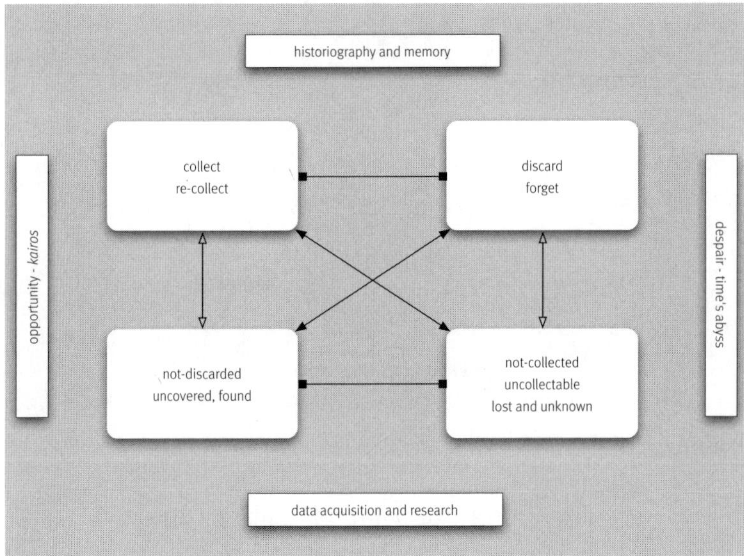

Figure 23 History and inspiration.

There are always choices to be made. The archaeologist cannot keep everything. Much of the past must be let go and consigned to the spoil heap. We cannot remember everything and must accept forgetting. "At a scene of crime anything might be relevant," and so the detective selects evidence on the basis of experience, hypothesis, or a hunch. I want to emphasize that the heart of figure 23 is the historical dynamic that Benjamin somewhat enigmatically elaborated in his *Theses on the Philosophy of History,* written at the end of his life in 1940. History's debris, discarded, forgotten fragments, lost in a deep abyss of time, require the work, suggested in the diagram, of (re)collection, of recovery (non-discard), discovering, finding. A key Latin term here is *invenire*—usually translated as "find," invenire includes both discovery *and* invention (the contradiction of discard and forgetting). Invention, innovation, creativity, and inspiration: breathing new life into the remains of the past.

At the heart is the historiographical temporality of actuality—the conjunction of past and present, in a moment of crisis, for Benjamin, with a view to changing the future. This is what Benjamin, in his *Theses on the Philosophy of History* (1970, written in 1940), called *Jetztzeit,* now-time, a conjunctural moment when the continuum of history is blown apart, when we take a stand against empty homogenous time in constructing a unique relationship now with the past. So Benjamin's *Thesis VI* opens: "Articulating the past historically does not mean recognizing it the way it really was. It means appropriating a memory as it flashes up in a moment of danger," when "the true image of the past flits by" (*Thesis V*)—when historical truth depends upon the work of connection at an appropriate opportunity. I have been using the term *kairos* for this, as well as actuality: the moment of invention. Historical articulation of this kind requires constant *creative* work, because the line of least resistance is for the past to be assimilated into familiar and comforting stories of progress: "every age must strive anew to wrest tradition away from the conformism that is working to overpower it" (*Thesis V*). The power of the past is to prompt reflection and action to redeem erstwhile hopes that may be lost in a tide of so-called progress, forgotten in clichés and formulaic, ideological accounts.

Figure 24 counterposes the surface of the land with a line across it: Hadrian's Wall and the Military Road, for example. The contradictions

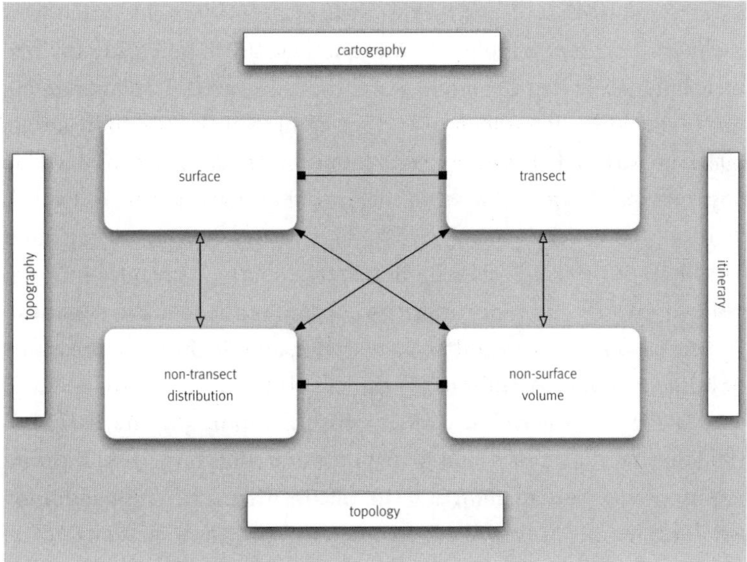

Figure 24 Chorography: place and region.

or negations reveal the connections with the topological representation found in chorographers like Wallis, and in Scott's work, too. While cartography handles the geometry of surfaces and lines across them, other kinds of representation are required for volumes and distributions of people, places and events. An itinerary, the description of a perambulation along a road, is one kind of representation of a transect through a region that reveals the folding of people and place/event.

There is no definitive end to these diagrams. Another set might follow the line of life, death and the abject, for example. I like the way that they graphically summarize the *creative* choices and pathways that may be taken through this field of the archaeological imagination. One thing does seem particularly clear to me: the institutionalization of archaeology, particularly in the state museums of the nineteenth century, involved a settling of pathways as others were marginalized. Choices were shut down. This is another way of pointing out that the archaeological, or antiquarian, imagination is far wider than what is now the discipline of archaeology.

4. The Archaeological Imagination

Voice; presence and loss; an elegiac moment; repair; hopes and utopias; anxieties over authenticity and fakery; the abject real; place and engagement; time, the past, future and actuality, and times beyond comprehension; the relationship between real and mediated, source and document; figures of the poet, ethnographer, scientist, collector, connoisseur, witness, as well as chorographer and ichnographer, plotters of places and ghosts; the role of speculation and inspiration; craft and its tools. These are some of the themes that have emerged as I have explored an archaeological sensibility and the work of the archaeological imagination.

Reviewing the genealogy of engagements with land and community in the predisciplinary eighteenth century reveals the subtlety of the political negotiation over the voice and authority of the author in relation to a chosen constituency, and the different ways of engaging history and the materiality of the past, many of which have been lost in modernist crystallization of disciplines and genres. Central to

---

The Archaeological Imagination by Michael Shanks, 145–150.

my review has been the concept of *performance,* with its wide valency. Engagements with place, land and the relics of the past; the work of writing and illustration, through walking and riding; the tools or props of measurement and documentation such as pencil, notebook, pocketwatch, camera lucida; the materialities of manuscript, voice and song, boots, horses, wheelchairs. I hope to have shown in my short examples how new insights can be gained by locating text and author in such practices, performances, and their accoutrement, as a complement to conventional commentary (see Rosemary Sweet's *Antiquaries* [2004] for a recent and orthodox treatment of antiquarianism as a contained intellectual field; contrast Martin Myron and Lucy Peltz's *Producing the Past: Aspects of Antiquarian Culture and Practice 1700–1850* [1999]). I have also been taken up by the theme of arrangement and architecture, landscape, too, in the disposition of people, artifacts and places, whether it is in the antiquarian's study, or the construction of landscapes.

As a summary, I offer the following components of an archaeological sensibility and imagination. There are three groups: *chora* (I prefer the Greek term over site or place, because it refers to people's inhabitation of a place), collection, and metamorphosis.

Chora

- Engagement. Archaeology establishes relationships—modes of engagement with the remains of the past. These are architectural and performative paradigms.
- Topology. Senses of place. This includes the topological folding of time inherent in our perception of site or place, as old things mingle with new.
- Place/event. This involves a fascination with the connection between place and event and is captured in the notion—*this happened here.*
- Forensic suspicion. A particular forensic and suspicious attitude towards place—*at a scene of crime anything might be relevant.*
- Figure and ground. A forensic connection between place and event involves a task of distinguishing and sorting evidence from

irrelevancy, what is significant from what is garbage, signal from noise, *figure from ground*. Sometimes this is a kind of cryptography.

Collection

- Sorting things out. Archaeologists are often concerned with classification, choosing what goes with what, in sorting finds, in making a significant collection, in deciding what matters over what is irrelevant (cf. figure and ground).
- Identity and recognition. *Is this the way we were?*—there is a crucial component of identity and identification, of recognition in archaeology. Are these are our ancestral traces?—there may be involved an uncanny sense of a haunting past.
- The real and the abject. Archaeological objects can never be completely captured in a description. There is always more to be said. Just as there is always an uneasy sense of ultimate mortality in archaeological engagements, that we, too, will one day be the dust of decay.
- The decisive moment. The temporality of discovery and recognition is *kairos* or actuality, the conjunction of two times, then and now, or the notion of a right time or opportunity. The decisive moment may be that of discovery—when the treasure of the past is recovered, or when the pieces of the puzzle come together, or the way the past, introduced into the present, can make us think freshly about the future.
- Endurance. Things can endure: it is material resistance to decay and entropy that connects past, present and future. Sometimes this is an active negative entropy: people, for example, can maintain and care for things so that they resist decay.
- *Mise-en-scène*. The arrangement of things in place to fit the interest of viewing and inspection is a key component of archaeological work, whether it be the trench section cleaned for scrutiny, a reconstruction of a building, or an assemblage of artifacts in a museum. Consider also the idea of landscape as a way of looking and arranging things in place.

Metamorphosis

- Ruin and phantasm. Archaeology works through remains and vestiges; bits remaining of the past as well as traces or tracks, impacts and imprints. It deals in a past which is not so much over and done, no longer present, as both present in ruins and remains and uncannily non-absent phantasms, hauntingly present.
- Archaeology and Ichnology. Traces, ruins and remains require Archaeology. Vestiges that witness the non-absence of the past require Ichnology—a science of vestiges.
- Displacement. Archaeology deals in displacement as a fundamental feature of representation—the shift from past to present, the circulation of text and image beyond the findspot, beyond the site whence the photo was taken, the re-location, citation, quotation of the image, document and account.
- Aftermath. *What comes after the event?* To document, repair, restore, conserve, replicate?
- Entropy. Ruin and decay and other metamorphic processes—*what becomes of what was.*
- Care. People do often care for things such that they resist loss and ruin (cf. Endurance).
- Representation. How can materiality—site, practice and thing—be documented?
- Alchemy and technology. The magic of past reappearing in the present. Archaeology has long included a technical fascination with recovery and reconstruction, with the technology of reproduction/documentation. This may even verge on technophilia—a love of the technology of recovery and reconstruction for its own sake.
- Worldbuilding. Modeling worlds on the basis of fragments.
- Hopes and utopias. Archaeological projects are always future oriented and frequently reference utopias, balancing realities and conjectures.

I wish to end on something of a dark note. My Borders anecdotes reveal clearly that the archaeological imagination is intimately associated with the cultural politics of property, land, identity and belonging, and voice, who gets access to the past and whose voice is heard. Eighteenth and nineteenth century antiquarians were all wealthy and northern European. The archaeological imagination is far from innocent. It is equally clear that there are many creative choices to be made in the way that we may take up the past. For me, at the heart of the archaeological imagination is *creative* practice that cuts across science and the humanities, the past and the present. There thus is an accompanying exhortation—to look beyond the academic discipline of archaeology through memory practices, tradition and innovation to a (modern) human condition and to find ways that the archaeological imagination may enhance and enrich human experience now and for the future.

References

I have made much use of the Oxford Dictionary of National Biography (Oxford University Press 2002).

Adorno, Theodor, and Max Horkheimer. 1979. *Dialectic of Enlightenment.* London: Verso.

Beck, Ulrich. 1992. *Risk Society: Towards a New Modernity.* London: Sage.

Bender, Barbara, Sue Hamilton, Christopher Y. Tilley, and Ed Anderson. 2007. *Stone Worlds: Narrative and Reflexivity in Landscape Archaeology.* Walnut Creek, CA: Left Coast Press, Inc.

Benjamin, Walter. 1970. Theses on the philosophy of history, in *Illuminations.* London: Jonathan Cape.

Burke, James. 2000. Circles*: 50 Round Trips Through History, Technology, Science, Culture.* New York: Simon & Schuster.

Burnett-Brown, Anthony, Michael Gray, and Russell Roberts. 2000. *Specimens and Marvels: Willam Henry Fox Talbot and the Invention of Photography.* New York: Aperture.

Butterfield, Herbert. 1931. *The Whig Interpretation of History.* London: G. Bell and Sons.

Cacciari, Massimo, and Germano Celant. 1997. *Anselm Kiefer.* Milan: Charta.

Clack, Timothy, and Marcus Brittain, eds. 2007. *Archaeology and the Media.* Walnut Creek, CA: Left Coast Press, Inc.

Clarke, David. 1973. Archaeology: the loss of innocence. *Antiquity* 47:6–18.

Culler, Jonathan. 1976. *Saussure.* London: Fontana Collins.

Daniel, Glyn Edmund. 1950. *A Hundred Years of Archaeology.* London: Duckworth.

The Archaeological Imagination by Michael Shanks, 151–158.

Davenport-Hines, R. P. T. 1998. *Gothic: Four Hundred Years of Excess, Horror, Evil, And Ruin*. London: Fourth Estate.

Downing, Eric. 2006. *After Images: Photography, Archaeology, and Psychoanalysis and the Tradition of Bildung*. Detroit: Wayne State University Press.

Finn, Christine. 2001. *Artifacts: An Archaeologist's Year in Silicon Valley*. Cambridge, MA: MIT Press.

———. 2004. *Past Poetic: Archaeology in the Poetry of W.B. Yeats and Seamus Heaney*. London: Duckworth.

Foucault, Michel. 1972. *The Archaeology of Knowledge*. London: Tavistock/Routledge.

———. 1989. *The Order of Things. An Archaeology of the Human Sciences*. London: Tavistock/Routledge.

Fox Talbot, and William Henry. 1844–46. *The Pencil of Nature*. London: Longman, Brown, Green and Longmans.

Freud, Sigmund. 2003 (1919). *The Uncanny*. Harmondsworth, UK: Penguin.

Gell, William. 1804. *The topography of Troy, and its vicinity; illustrated and explained by drawings and descriptions*. London: T.N. Longman and O. Rees.

———. 1807. *The geography and antiquities of Ithaca*. London: Printed by J. Wright for Longman, Hurst, Rees, and Orme.

———. 1810. *The Itinerary of Greece, with a commentary on Pausanias and Strabo, and an account of the Monuments of Antiquity at present existing in that country, compiled in the years 1801, 2, 5, 6 etc*. London: T. Payne.

———, and John Gandy. 1824. *Pompeiana. The Topography, Edifices, and Ornaments of Pompeii*. London: Rodwell and Martin.

Gianacchi, Gabriella, Nick Kaye, and Michael Shanks, eds. 2012. *Archaeologies of Presence*. London: Routledge.

Giddens, Anthony. 1991. *Modernity and Self-Identity: Self and Society in the Late Modern Age*. Cambridge, UK: Blackwell Polity.

Gordon, Alexander. 1726. *Itinerarium septentrionale: or, A journey thro' most of the counties of Scotland, and those in the north of England. In two parts ... illustrated with sixty-six copper plates*. London: Printed for the author and sold by G. Strahan etc.

Gregory, Derek. 1994. *Geographical Imaginations*. Oxford, UK: Blackwell.

Greimas, A.J. 1983. *Structural Semantics: An Attempt at a Method*. Lincoln: Nebraska University Press.

———, and François Rastier. 1968. The interaction of semiotic constraints. *Yale French Studies* 41:86–105.

Hall, Peter. 1998. *Cities in Civilization: Culture, Innovation, and Urban Order.* London: Weidenfeld & Nicolson.

Harvey, David. 1969. *Explanation in Geography.* London: Edward Arnold.

———. 1973. *Social Justice and the City.* London: Edward Arnold.

Hauser, Kitty. 2007. *Shadow Sites: Photography, Archaeology, and the British Landscape, 1927–1955.* Oxford; New York: Oxford University Press.

Helgerson, Richard. 1995. Forms *of Nationhood: the Elizabethan Writing of England.* Chicago: University of Chicago Press.

Hewison, Robert. 1987. *The Heritage Industry: Britain in a Climate of Decline.* London: Methuen.

Hingley, Richard. 2008. *The Recovery of Roman Britain 1586–1906: A Colony so Fertile.* Oxford: Oxford University Press.

Hodder, Ian, ed. 1982. *Symbolic and Structural Archaeology.* Cambridge: Cambridge University Press.

Holtorf, Cornelius. 2005. *From Stonehenge to Las Vegas: Archaeology as Popular Culture.* Walnut Creek, CA: AltaMira Press.

———. 2007. *Archaeology is a Brand!: the Meaning of Archaeology in Contemporary Popular Culture.* Walnut Creek, CA: Left Coast Press, Inc.

Horsley, John. 1732. *Britannia Romana, or, The Roman Antiquities of Britain.* London: Printed for J. Osborn and T. Longman.

Hutchinson, William. 1778. *A View of Northumberland, with an Excursion to the Abbey of Mailross in Scotland.* Newcastle: Printed by T. Saint by W. Charnley, Vesey and Whitfield.

Hutton, James. 1788. *Theory of the earth; or, An investigation of the laws observable in the composition, dissolution, and restoration of land upon the globe.* Edinburgh.

———. 1788. Theory of the earth, or, an investigation of the laws observable in the composition, dissoultion, and restoration of land upon the globe. *Transactions of the Royal Society of Edinburgh* 1:209–304.

———. 1794. *An Investigation of the principles of knowledge and of the progress of reason, from sense to science and philosophy.* London: A. Strahan and T. Cadell.

Hutton, William. 1781. *An History of Birmingham to the end of the year 1780.* Birmingham: Pearson.

———. 1802. *History of the Roman Wall, which crosses the island of Britain from the German Ocean to the Irish Sea. Describing its Ancient State, and its Appearance in the Year 1801.* London: John Nichols etc.

———, and Catherine Hutton. 1841. *The life of William Hutton, stationer, of Birmingham; and the history of his family.* London: C. Knight and Co.

Jessop, Ronald. 1961. *Curiosities of British Archaeology*. London: Butterworths.

Johanson, Donald C., and Blake Edgar. 1996. *From Lucy to Language*. New York: Simon & Schuster.

Kaye, Nick. 2000. *Site-specific Art: Performance, Place and Documentation*. London; New York: Routledge.

Latour, Bruno, and Shirley Strum. 1986. Human social origins: Oh please, tell us another story!, . *Journal of Social and Biological Structures* 9:169–87.

Lenoir, Timothy. 1994. Was that last turn a right turn? The semiotic turn and A.J. Greimas. *Configurations* 2:119–36.

Lewis, Matthew Gregory. 1808. *Romantic Tales*. London: Longman, Hurst, Rees, and Orme.

Lockhart, John Gibson. 1850. *Memoirs of the Life of Sir Walter Scott, Bart*. Edinburgh: Cadell.

Lowenthal, David. 1985. *The Past is a Foreign Country*. Cambridge: Cambridge University Press.

Macpherson, James. 1765. *The Works of Ossian, the Son of Fingal*. London: Printed for T.Becket and P.A. Dehondt.

Miller, Peter N. 2000. *Peiresc's Europe: Learning and Virtue in the Seventeenth Century*. New Haven, CT: Yale University Press.

Mills, C. Wright. 1959. *The Sociological Imagination*. New York: Oxford University Press.

Myrone, Martin, and Lucy Peltz. 1999. *Producing the Past: Aspects of Antiquarian Culture and Practice, 1700–1850*. Brookfield, VT: Ashgate.

Neville, Brian, and Johanne Villeneuve, eds. 2002. *Waste-Site Stories: The Recycling of Memory*. Albany, NY: SUNY.

Olivier, Laurent. 2008. *Le sombre abîme du temps: mémoire et archeologie*. Paris: Seuil.

———. 2012. *The Dark Abyss of Time: Archaeology and Memory*. Lanham, MD: AltaMira Press.

Olsen, Bjørnar, Michael Shanks, Timothy Webmoor, and Christopher Witmore. 2012. *Archaeology: the Discipline of Things*. Berkeley: University of California Press.

Palmer, Roy. 2004. Percy, Thomas (1729–1811). *Oxford Dictionary of National Biography*. Oxford: Oxford University Press.

Pearson, Mike. 2007. *In Comes I: Performance, Memory, and Landscape*. Exeter: University of Exeter Press.

———, and Michael Shanks. 2001. *Theatre/Archaeology*. London: Routledge.

Percy, Thomas. 1765. *Reliques of Ancient English Poetry*. London: Printed for J. Dodsley.

Piggott, Stuart. 1950. *William Stukeley, an Eighteenth-century Antiquary*. Oxford, UK: Clarendon Press.

———. 1976. *Ruins in a Landscape: Essays in Antiquarianism*. Edinburgh: Edinburgh University Press.

Playfair, John. 1802. *Illustrations of the Huttonian Theory of the Earth*. Edinburgh: Cadell and Davies.

———. 1805. Biographical account of the late James Hutton, FRS Edinburgh. *Transactions of the Royal Society of Edinburgh* 5:39–99.

Poe, Edgar Allan. 1984. *Complete Stories and Poems*. New York: Doubleday.

Poovey, Mary. 1998. *A History of the Modern Fact: Problems of Knowledge in the Sciences of Wealth and Society*. Chicago: University of Chicago Press.

Prince, H.C. 1962. The geographical imagination. *Landscape* 11:22–5.

Propp, V. I. A. 1958 (1928). *Morphology of the Folktale*. Bloomington: Research Center, Indiana University.

Rathje, William L., and Cullen Murphy. 1992. *Rubbish!: the Archaeology of Garbage*. New York: HarperCollins Publishers.

Ritson, Joseph. 1782. *Observations on the three first volumes of The history of English poetry*. London: J. Stockdale etc.

———. 1783. *A Select Collection of English Songs*. London: Printed for J. Johnson.

———. 1791. *Pieces of Ancient Popular Poetry: from Authentic Manuscripts and Old Printed Copies*. London,: Printed by C. Clarke, for T. and J. Egerton.

———. 1792. *Ancient Songs, from the Time of King Henry the Third, to the Revolution*. London: Printed for J. Johnson.

———. 1820. *Robin Hood: a collection of all the ancient poems, songs, and ballads, now extant, relative to that celebrated English outlaw*. London: Printed for Longman, Hurst, Rees, Orme.

Salzani, Carlo. 2007. The city as crime scene: Walter Benjamin and the traces of the detective. *New German Critique* 34:165–87.

Schnapp, Alain. 1993. *La conquete du passé: aux origines de l'archéologie*. Paris: Carré.

———. 1996. *The Discovery of the Past: The Origins of Archaeology*. London: British Museum Press.

Schnapp, Jeffrey, Michael Shanks, and Matthew Tiews. 2004. Archaeologies of the Modern. *Modernism/Modernity* 11.

Scott, Walter. 1802. *Minstrelsy of the Scottish border: consisting of historical and romantic ballads*. Kelso: Printed by J. Ballantyne, for T. Cadell, jun. and W. Davies, London: etc.

———. 1814. *Border Antiquities of England and Scotland. Comprising Specimens of Architecture and Sculpture, and other vestiges of former ages, accompanied by descriptions. Together with Illustrations of remarkable incidents in Border History and tradition, and Original Poetry.* London: Longman, Hirst, Rees, etc.

———. 1836. *Tales of a Grandfather*. Edinburgh: R. Cadell.

———. 1890. *Poetical Works*. Boston and New York: Houghton Mifflin.

———. 2009 (1816). *Old Mortality*. Oxford: Oxford University Press.

Serres, Michel. 1995. *The Natural Contract*. Ann Arbor: University of Michigan Press.

Shanks, Michael. 1987. *Reconstructing Archaeology: Theory and Practice*. Cambridge: Cambridge University Press.

———. 1992. *Experiencing the Past: On the Character of Archaeology*. London: Routledge.

———. 1996. *Classical Archaeology: Experiences of the Discipline*. London: Routledge.

———, and Christopher Tilley. 1987. *Social Theory and Archaeology*. Albuquerque: University of New Mexico Press.

Shapin, S., and S. Schaffer. 1986. *Leviathan and the Air-Pump: Hobbes, Boyle and the Experimental Life*. Princeton, NJ: Princeton University Press.

Shelley, Percy Bysshe. 2004. *Complete Poetry*. Eds. Donald H Reiman and Neilm Fraistat. Baltimore: Johns Hopkins University Press.

Sloterdijk, Peter. 2004. *Sphären III: Schäume, Plurale Sphärolgie*. Frankfurt: Suhrkamp.

Solnit, Rebecca. 2000. *Wanderlust: a History of Walking*. New York: Viking.

Solnit, Rebecca, Ben Pease, and Shizue Siegel. 2010. *Infinite City: A San Francisco Atlas*. Berkeley: University of California Press.

Spooner, Catherine. 2007. *Contemporary Gothic*. London: Reaktion Books.

Stengers, Isabelle. 2005. Introductory notes on an ecology of practices. *Cultural Studies* 11:183–96.

———. 2010. *Cosmopolitics*. Minneapolis: University of Minnesota Press.

Stewart, Susan. 1991. *Crimes of Writing: Problems in the Containment of Representation*. New York: Oxford University Press.

Sultan, Larry, and Mike Mandel. 2004. *Evidence*. New York: Distributed Art Publishers.

Sweet, Rosemary. 2004. *Antiquaries: The Discovery of the Past in Eighteenth-Century Britain*. London: Hambledon and London.

Thomas, Julian. 2004. *Archaeology and Modernity*. London: Routledge.

Tilley, Christopher. 1994. *A Phenomenology of Landscape: Places, Paths and Monuments*. Oxford: Berg.

Trigger, Bruce. 1989. *A History of Archaeological Thought*. Cambridge: Cambridge University Press.

Wainwright, Clive. 1989. *The Romantic Interior: The British Collector at Home, 1750–1850*. New Haven, CT: Yale University Press.

Wallace, Jennifer. 2004. *Digging the Dirt: The Archaeological Imagination*. London: Duckworth.

Wallis, John. 1769. *The natural history and antiquities of Northumberland: and of so much of the county of Durham as lies between the rivers Tyne and Tweed; commonly called North Bishoprick*. London: Printed for the author by W. and W. Strahan.

Welford, Richard. 1895. *Men of Mark Twixt Tyne and Tweed*. London and Newcastle-upon-Tyne: Walter Scott.

White, Hayden. 1973. *Metahistory: The Historical Imagination in Nineteenth-Century Europe*. Baltimore: Johns Hopkins University Press.

Williams, Gilda, ed. 2007. The Gothic *(Whitechapel: Documents of Contemporary Art)*. Cambridge, MA: MIT Press.

Wordsworth, William, Samuel Taylor Coleridge, R. L. Brett, and Alun R. Jones. 2005. *Wordsworth and Coleridge: Lyrical Ballads*. London; New York: Routledge.

Zielinski, Siegfried. 2006. *Deep Time of the Media: Toward an Archaeology of Hearing and Seeing by Technical Means*. Cambridge, MA: MIT Press.

Index

The Archaeological Imagination by Michael Shanks, 159–166.

H

I

J

K

About the Author

Michael Shanks is the Omar and Althea Dwyer Hoskins Professor of Classical Archaeology at Stanford University. He has worked on the archaeology of early farmers in northern Europe, Greek cities in the Mediterranean, Roman landscapes, eighteenth-century antiquarians as well as the application of archaeology to the contemporary world. Metamedia, his archaeology lab at Stanford, has pioneered the use of new media and information technologies to facilitate collaborative interdisciplinary networks in researching design, heritage, memory practices and long-term historical trends. His books, including *ReConstructing Archaeology* (1987), *Social Theory and Archaeology* (1987), *Experiencing the Past* (1992), *Art and the Early Greek State* (1999) and *Theatre/Archaeology* (2001) have made him a key figure in contemporary archaeological thought. (See also michaelshanks.org.)

Left Coast Press, Inc. is committed to preserving ancient forests and natural resources. We elected to print this title on 30% post consumer recycled paper, processed chlorine free. As a result, for this printing, we have saved:

2 Trees (40' tall and 6-8" diameter)
1 Million BTUs of Total Energy
149 Pounds of Greenhouse Gases
671 Gallons of Wastewater
42 Pounds of Solid Waste

Left Coast Press, Inc. made this paper choice because our printer, Thomson-Shore, Inc., is a member of Green Press Initiative, a nonprofit program dedicated to supporting authors, publishers, and suppliers in their efforts to reduce their use of fiber obtained from endangered forests.

For more information, visit www.greenpressinitiative.org

Environmental impact estimates were made using the Environmental Defense Paper Calculator. For more information visit: www.papercalculator.org.